New Visions for Linking Literature and Mathematics

New Visions for Linking Literature and Mathematics

David J. Whitin
Wayne State University

Phyllis Whitin
Wayne State University

 National Council of Teachers of English
1111 W. Kenyon Road, Urbana, Illinois 61801-1096

National Council of Teachers of Mathematics
1906 Association Drive, Reston, Virginia 20191-1502

For permission credit lines, see Permissions Acknowledgments, page vi.

Staff Editor: Bonny Graham

Interior Design: Doug Burnett

Cover Design: Jenny Jensen Greenleaf

Cover photographs courtesy of the authors.

NCTE Stock Number: 33487-3050

NCTM Stock Number: 12777

It is the policy of NCTE in its journals and other publications to provide a forum for the open discussion of ideas concerning the content and the teaching of English and the language arts. Publicity accorded to any particular point of view does not imply endorsement by the Executive Committee, the Board of Directors, or the membership at large, except in announcements of policy, where such endorsement is clearly specified.

Library of Congress Cataloging-in-Publication Data

Whitin, David Jackman, 1947–
    New visions for linking literature and mathematics / David J. Whitin, Phyllis Whitin.
        p. cm.
Includes bibliographical references.
    ISBN 0-8141-3348-7 (pbk.)
    1. Mathematics—Study and teaching (Elementary) 2. Literature in mathematics education. I. Whitin, Phyllis. II. Title.
    QA135.6.W49 2004
    372.7—dc22

                                                          2003023544

To our best teachers

Dave

Brett

Becca

Permissions Acknowledgments

Contents

Foreword

The time is right for this book. Classroom teachers are increasingly aware that children's literature can contribute to the teaching of mathematics. But knowing this is one thing; acting on it is another, for it requires at the very least an enormous expenditure of the teacher's time as he or she finds and examines children's literature (a vast and ever-growing field) and then selects and incorporates the chosen books wisely and well. David and Phyllis Whitin offer help with all of this. They know children's literature well, having examined it closely and comprehensively. They recommend the titles they find most promising and tell us why, and they share numerous actual classroom examples of teachers using selected books in ways that actualize their mathematics and literary potential for children's engagement.

So much comes together in this book. Literature and mathematics do indeed "link," as the title promises they will.

- They link in the selected math-related children's books these authors discuss.
- They link in the suggestions the authors provide for engaging children with this literature.
- They link in the many actual examples of children's talk and writing that build on this literature.
- They link in the authors' explicit anchoring of their discussion and recommendations in two sets of Standards: English language arts and mathematics.

But literature and mathematics aren't all that get linked in this book. David and Phyllis Whitin also unite the theoretical and the practical. This is hardly surprising in a book by researchers who are also teachers. The authors have lived much of their professional lives in classrooms, not only as observers but also as players—the ones who plan and implement and initiate and respond and get frustrated and wonder why and back up and try again. Teachers. Of course, they are researchers too: questioning, observing, gathering data (children's and teachers' talk and writing), making sense of what they gather, always connecting their own work with the ongoing work of other researchers. And so they know and live and—fortunately for us—share their vast and deep knowledge of the "field" (theory) and of the classroom. Because their lived experience has encompassed both theory and practice, we trust them to bring us a book that is theoretically grounded but in which the theory plays out in the realities of classroom life: What math-related children's books are out there? Which are the most promising? For what ages? Focusing on what math concepts? Incorporating what literary features? How might I engage the children with these books in ways that build on their mathematical and literary possibilities? In dealing with these matters, the book enables both teachers and children.

Teachers and children—a third linking in this book. We hear the actual talk of teachers and children as they engage in a variety of activities incorporating math-related children's literature. And we see abundant examples of children's written products. But whether we see the example or hear it, we are ever aware that it comes from a classroom community of teachers and children working and playing together with math-related children's literature.

I find it interesting to reflect on this book in relation to the criteria the authors suggest for evaluating math-related children's literature. They seek children's books that:

- have mathematical *integrity:* content that is accurate, accessible, and clear and that promotes positive attitudes toward mathematics. *New Visions for Linking Literature and Mathematics* has this integrity. Its foundation is NCTM's *Principles and Standards for School Mathematics* (2000), Standards that articulate our best current thinking about the teaching of mathematics. The integrity is evident, too, in the lucid and engaging presentation that enhances the reader's understanding.

- have potential for *varied response. New Visions* has this potential, for it invites the reader to enter the text in many ways. This book informs, it piques curiosity, it excites imagination (as in imagining how events like those the authors describe might play out in one's own classroom).

- have an *aesthetic* dimension. The aesthetic dimension in *New Visions* is both visual and verbal. The graphics—diagrams, sidebars, children's written products—are not simply decorative but rather are integral to and supportive of the text. And the written text itself is well crafted in its organization, fluency, and clarity.

- are *inclusive* of race, culture, and gender. For me, a particularly striking example of this inclusiveness in *New Visions* comes in the authors' discussion of book pairing. The book pairings include Chinese, Chinese American, African, African American, and other international settings, and several have female protagonists. This is but one example in a book that resounds with an appreciation of human diversity.

That *New Visions* meets the authors' criteria for excellence is significant for, as any writer knows, meeting one's own standard of excellence is the author's most formidable challenge of all.

I like the "voicefulness" of this text. When I read it, I hear the voices of teachers and children. I hear the authors' voices too, voices that convey their own sense of wonder and excitement about using math-related children's literature in the classroom. Their excitement is contagious, and I think you just may come away from your reading of this enabling, linking book thinking, "Yes, my students and I can do this. I'm gonna give it a try."

—Judith Lindfors
Professor Emerita, University of Texas at Austin

Introduction

This book is about math-related literature and how to use it effectively in the elementary classroom. It is a book *for* teachers because it came *from* teachers. It is teachers who showed us the mathematical possibilities of math-related literature by connecting it to the lives of their students. It is teachers who discovered the language arts potential of these same books, as their students used the predictability of mathematical patterns and the clues from illustrations to make sense of these texts. And it is teachers who remarked that using the same literature book in both literacy and mathematics blocks allowed them to effectively address curricular objectives in each of these areas.

We have also had discussions with teachers about how to appropriately select math-related literature. Because of the ever-increasing number of such books on the market, we felt it was important to begin this book with an examination of criteria for evaluating math-related literature. We have linked these criteria to the National Council of Teachers of Mathematics' (NCTM) *Principles and Standards for School Mathematics* (2000) and the National Council of Teachers of English (NCTE) and the International Reading Association's (IRA) *Standards for the English Language Arts* (1996). Highlighting the Standards from both organizations draws attention to the many parallels between them. Both make explicit the importance of reasoning and communicating effectively through writing, talking, and graphic representation. It is our intent that this tying together of both sets of Standards will help teachers justify the decisions they make as they integrate curriculum.

The next three chapters explore effective strategies for using these books with students. In Chapter 2, "Books for a Wide Range of Ages," we show how the same book is used by teachers of many different grade levels, emphasizing how good books have a range of applicability in terms of grade level and mathematical/language arts possibilities. In Chapter 3, "Problem Posing with Children's Literature," we again use specific classroom examples, this time to demonstrate how fruitful extension activities can emerge from children's own questions and observations. In Chapter 4, "Using the Strategy of Book Pairs," we discuss how teachers select two math-related books that provide an interesting comparison and contrast, sharing a range of books and grade-level examples to demonstrate the wide applicability of this strategy. We conclude each of these chapters with a list of additional books for teachers to investigate further.

Finally, in Chapter 5, "Best Books for Exploring," we provide an annotated list of the best math-related literature available, as well as suggestions for introducing these books to children.

Having described what this book *is*, let's take a moment to clarify what this book is *not*. First, this book is *not* intended as an entire mathematics or literacy program. At the same time, the experiences we describe are not "enrichment activities" to be added to an already crammed schedule.

We expect that you, like the teachers in this book, will use the books discussed here for a variety of purposes. Some of these purposes include:

- To introduce a mathematical concept or to assess your students' prior experience and knowledge: What do my students know about fractions? What language do they use to describe fractional situations? What personal experiences do they describe when they hear this story?

- To address mathematical misconceptions: Why is 1/8 < 1/2? How is perimeter different from area?

- To show another representation of a mathematical idea, such as counting-on by a multiple versus an array (area) model of multiplication.

- To examine the author's craft and purpose across a wide range of genres.

- To inspire meaningful research and support a variety of individual and collaborative pieces of writing.

Second, we offer the activities in this book *not* as prescriptions to follow but as possibilities to adapt and explore. As you begin to envision these possibilities and plan investigations with your own students, we invite you to consider these questions:

- What are my curricular objectives and standards?

- How might mathematical experiences cross over into language arts, social studies, or science blocks?

- What kind of experiences can I manage most successfully? Do I have the resources that are necessary? How can I adapt this book or activity to fit my own teaching situation?

- When my students hear and view a book, what seems to intrigue them the most? What do they ask questions about? How do their responses tie to other curricular areas?

Just as teachers provided the spark for our writing of this book, we're confident that you and your students will adapt and transform these strategies in exciting new ways. We hope to hear from you.

References   National Council of Teachers of English and International Reading Associa-
                  tion. *Standards for the English Language Arts*. Urbana, IL: National
                  Council of Teachers of English, 1996.

                  National Council of Teachers of Mathematics. *Principles and Standards for
                  School Mathematics*. Reston, VA: National Council of Teachers of
                  Mathematics, 2000.

1

Criteria for Selecting Math-Related Books

I t's exciting to visit the exhibit areas of mathematics and language arts conferences these days. Baskets of math-related books beckon us from publishers' booths. We mentally calculate how much our budgets will allow, or how much weight we can bear to carry, as we browse the displays. Just a dozen or so years ago, this scenario would not have occurred. Several factors have contributed to the current interest in integrating literature and mathematics. When the National Council of Teachers of Mathematics (NCTM) first published *Curriculum and Evaluation Standards for School Mathematics* (1989), the role of written and oral communication in promoting mathematical understanding gained new attention. At the same time, literature-based reading programs gained popularity. Soon several resources for teachers (Burns 1992; Whitin and Wilde 1992, 1995) appeared that elaborated on the benefits of using stories as real-life contexts for mathematical ideas; they named specific books that inspire mathematical exploration and outlined strategies for using those books with children. Most mathematics textbook series began to include suggestions for links to literature or provided copies of children's books as part of ancillary materials. More recently, NCTM published *Principles and Standards for School Mathematics* (2000), which further articulates the role of communication in mathematics.

Authors and publishers capitalized on this opportunity to link literature and mathematics. Over the years, the market has been increasingly flooded with hundreds of titles. Not all of these books, however, are of equal quality. Many math-related books seem more like workbooks than stories (Austin 1998; Whitin and Whitin 2001). Some give detailed prescriptions for reading, much like a teaching manual for a basal reader, while others mask doses of "skills" with comical illustrations or popular food products to "motivate" young learners. Others claim to be aligned with the NCTM Standards but with little or no substantiated evidence. Faced with this situation, educators today need specific tools with which to evaluate books for classroom use. In this chapter, we define and explain criteria from two different perspectives: the mathematical and the language arts. We base our discussion of the mathematical perspective on an opening overview of the Principles and Standards. Next we examine the ways all the criteria apply to one book, *If You Hopped Like a Frog* (Schwartz 1999). Finally, we describe in depth a range of books that specifically exemplify each of the criteria as well as those that do not. Through this illustrated discussion of the book selection process, we set the stage for discussing effective ways of engaging children with that literature.

The Criteria

First and foremost, math-related books should be good *literature*. Both fiction and nonfiction books of good quality engage, inspire, and delight young readers yet appeal to adults as well. They beg rereading. When illustrated, a book's pictures and graphics complement and extend the text. Good books are inclusive by valuing, portraying, and drawing in readers of all ethnicities, cultures, and genders.

You might be saying to yourself at this point, "These are the factors I consider when I choose good read-alouds or books for my classroom library." Absolutely! When selecting and evaluating math-related literature, we begin with these crucial elements. We then specify criteria that focus on mathematics: that books convey sound and accurate content and that they promote healthy attitudes and dispositions about mathematics. Since the mathematical features distinguish these criteria from more general ones, we devote a large part of this chapter to examining these dimensions in depth. We invite you also to keep in mind the implications of our discussion for meeting the National Council of Teachers of English (NCTE) and International Reading Association (IRA) Standards for the English language arts (Table 1.1), such as reading and writing a wide variety of genres for different purposes; examining authors' and illustrators' craft; interpreting graphs, charts, and other visual formats; and so forth. In other words, we want you to explore with us the reciprocal benefit of using math-related literature to strengthen both your language arts and mathematics classrooms.

Summarizing the preceding discussion, we offer the following criteria as a guide. We believe that good math-related books for children should demonstrate:

1. *Mathematical integrity:* The mathematical components of the book are accurate. In fiction, the mathematics reflects functional use in believable contexts. The ideas and concepts in all genres are accessible to the reader. The tone of the book promotes healthy mathematical attitudes and dispositions.

Table 1.1
NCTE/IRA Standards for
the English Language Arts

1. Students read a wide range of print and nonprint texts to build an understanding of texts, of themselves, and of the cultures of the United States and the world; to acquire new information; to respond to the needs and demands of society and the workplace; and for personal fulfillment. Among these texts are fiction and nonfiction, classic and contemporary works.

2. Students read a wide range of literature from many periods in many genres to build an understanding of the many dimensions (e.g., philosophical, ethical, aesthetic) of human experience.

3. Students apply a wide range of strategies to comprehend, interpret, evaluate, and appreciate texts. They draw on their prior experience, their interactions with other readers and writers, their knowledge of word meaning and of other texts, their word identification strategies, and their understanding of textual features (e.g., sound-letter correspondence, sentence structure, context, graphics).

4. Students adjust their use of spoken, written, and visual language (e.g., conventions, style, vocabulary) to communicate effectively with a variety of audiences and for different purposes.

5. Students employ a wide range of strategies as they write and use different writing process elements appropriately to communicate with different audiences for a variety of purposes.

6. Students apply knowledge of language structure, language conventions (e.g., spelling and punctuation), media techniques, figurative language, and genre to create, critique, and discuss print and nonprint texts.

7. Students conduct research on issues and interests by generating ideas and questions, and by posing problems. They gather, evaluate, and synthesize data from a variety of sources (e.g., print and nonprint texts, artifacts, people) to communicate their discoveries in ways that suit their purpose and audience.

8. Students use a variety of technological and informational resources (e.g., libraries, databases, computer networks, video) to gather and synthesize information and to create and communicate knowledge.

9. Students develop an understanding of and respect for diversity in language use, patterns, and dialects across cultures, ethnic groups, geographic regions, and social roles.

10. Students whose first language is not English make use of their first language to develop competency in the English language arts and to develop understanding of content across the curriculum.

11. Students participate as knowledgeable, reflective, creative, and critical members of a variety of literacy communities.

12. Students use spoken, written, and visual language to accomplish their own purposes (e.g., for learning, enjoyment, persuasion, and the exchange of information).

National Council of Teachers of English and International Reading Association. *Standards for the English Language Arts.* Urbana, IL: National Council of Teachers of English and Newark, DE: International Reading Association, 1996, p. 3.

2. *Potential for varied response:* The tone of the book is invitational rather than didactic.

3. *An aesthetic dimension:* The book heightens the reader's awareness and appreciation of form and design. The language and/or the illustrations appeal to the reader's senses and emotions. The design and format of informational graphics (charts, tables, graphs) are visually pleasing and pique young readers' interest. Visual material complements and extends the text.

4. *Ethnic, gender, and cultural inclusiveness:* The content, language, and illustrations promote racial, cultural, and gender equity. There are no instances of stereotyping or tokenism. Cultural representations are authentic.

Before examining these criteria more closely and describing books that exemplify them, as well as some that don't, we give a brief overview of NCTM's *Principles and Standards for School Mathematics* (2000). Familiarity with this document lays the foundation for evaluating books for their mathematical integrity as well as the other criteria.

A Brief Look at NCTM's Principles and Standards

NCTM developed *Principles and Standards for School Mathematics* (2000) in order to identify and describe features of mathematics education for today's world. First, the document addresses the need for this vision, stressing that *all* children need to learn mathematics with understanding and be able to use it in everyday life (p. 4). In the twenty-first century, it is not sufficient for children simply to be able to perform rote operations. Being mathematically literate today means being able to solve complex problems, make decisions through evaluating alternatives, and communicate effectively. Society is increasingly mathematical and technological. Citizens are bombarded with statistical information in the news media and in the workplace. Voters must make sense of financial information in the billions (and trillions) and comprehend the implications of economic decisions for international relations. Consumers face a multitude of purchasing and investment decisions. An ever-widening range of careers involves mathematical thinking, problem solving, and the use of technological tools. Mathematics and technology affect leisure time: recreation, the arts, and travel. The future of our planet depends on an understanding of issues such as global warming and the distribution of resources. Given the degree to which mathematics permeates today's world, excellence in mathematics cannot be reserved for an elite few.

NCTM developed six Principles, five Content Standards, and five Process Standards to describe this excellence in mathematics education. As you read through the following three lists, we invite you to consider the potential of children's literature to address the Principles and Standards.

Principles

- The Equity Principle: High expectations and strong support for all permeate the mathematics program.
- The Curriculum Principle: The curriculum is well developed and articulated throughout the grades; various strands of mathematics are integrated.
- The Teaching Principle: Teachers understand what students know, what they need to know, and support them in their learning by developing the classroom environment.
- The Learning Principle: Students demonstrate understanding, connect and apply mathematical ideas, and exhibit key attitudes and dispositions of mathematical thinkers.
- The Assessment Principle: Assessment informs instruction and learning; assessment benefits both teachers and students.
- The Technology Principle: Technology impacts and enhances both teaching and learning.

Content Standards

- Number and Operations: This strand includes numbers, ways of representing numbers, relationships among numbers, and number systems. Flexible use of strategies is a key part of computational fluency.
- Algebra: Algebraic thinking spans all grades. It includes experience with understanding, representing, and analyzing patterns, relations, and functions.
- Geometry: This strand encompasses analysis of two- and three-dimensional geometric shapes, spatial relationships and their representations, symmetry, transformation, and geometric problem solving.
- Measurement: This strand includes understanding measurable attributes, the units, systems, and processes of measurement, and flexible use of tools and strategies.
- Data Analysis and Probability: This strand addresses the collection of data, its representation and interpretation. Probability is a key part of data analysis as well as a dimension of many other areas of mathematics.

Process Standards

- Problem Solving: Students identify and solve problems that arise from a variety of experiences and encompass connected mathematical ideas. They analyze problems and apply a wide range of strategies in flexible ways.

- Reasoning and Proof: Students make conjectures (informed guesses), express these conjectures in multiple ways (through language and other forms of representation), and analyze and evaluate their reasonableness.

- Communication: Students organize their thinking by expressing their ideas clearly, and by considering and analyzing the ideas of others. Students use the language of mathematics effectively.

- Connections: Students recognize the connections among mathematical ideas and across experiences. They acknowledge, appreciate, and apply mathematical ideas outside the mathematics curriculum.

- Representation: Representation is both a process (to represent) and a product (or artifact). Representations include such forms as symbols, pictures, charts, models, and graphic displays. Representations are not ends in themselves, but tools for understanding and communication.

The Principles and Standards connect to our four criteria for evaluating math-related books in many ways. The Content Standards serve as a guide for considering the range of mathematical topics to identify in literature. Good books can promote the Process Standards by incorporating a variety of representations (illustrations, charts, models, etc.), showing mathematics in interdisciplinary contexts, and, most important, inviting children to talk, reason, and solve problems in multiple ways. Good books embody the Principles by fostering positive attitudes and dispositions toward mathematics and by providing an inclusive context for all children to discuss and explore mathematical ideas. In addition, these discussions and explorations can give teachers opportunities to assess their students' understandings.

Have you noticed some surprising parallels between the goals of NCTM and the NCTE/IRA Standards? Both documents, for instance, stress communication (NCTE/IRA Standard 4; NCTM Process Standard, Communication). They acknowledge that effective communication develops through multiple experiences using written, spoken, and visual language in a variety of contexts and purposes. Both mathematics and language are viewed as tools for meeting the demands of everyday life: to acquire information, to participate in society (NCTE/IRA Standard 1), to identify and solve problems in a variety of experiences (NCTM Process Standard, Problem Solving), and to connect ideas across experiences (NCTM Process Standard, Connections; NCTE/IRA Standards 7, 11).

With these ideas in mind, we turn to a discussion of specific pieces of literature to explore how these books reflect the criteria and the beliefs that undergird them.

Examining One Book in Depth

We've selected one math-related book, *If You Hopped Like a Frog* by David M. Schwartz (1999), in order to examine its classroom potential, using the criteria as a lens. Schwartz opens the book with a letter to the reader in which he describes his boyhood fascination with a frog's ability to leap: "I imagined soaring through the air with grace and ease, landing gently on my big, springy legs. How far could I hop?" (Unpaged). This hypothetical situation, as well as

"How far can you hop if you hopped like a frog?" ✱

Talk about Math & Comparing but makes you think of real life / and other situations

- Type of book that kids would ask many ???

other musings about the attributes and abilities of animals, became challenging problems for Schwartz to solve with some reasoning and research: "Once you know that a frog can jump twenty times its body length, you can figure out how far you could hop if you hopped like a frog." In the text that follows, Schwartz names a variety of other animals and their special adaptations and playfully imagines humans with proportional powers. With the strength of an ant, for example, a child could lift a car. It would be possible for humans to see a moving rabbit from "high in the clouds" if only they had the vision of an eagle. Having the capacity of a pelican's beak for a mouth would enable a person to drink a "triple root beer float in one mouthful." James Warhola's comical illustrations make these and other imaginative scenarios come to life. In the endnotes following the story, Schwartz describes and defends his problem-solving procedures and invites the reader to try these ideas or extend them in new ways. He explains, for example, that an eagle owes its sharp vision to the fact that it has 1,000,000 cones per square millimeter of retina, whereas a human has only 200,000. Therefore, an eagle can see a moving rabbit from a distance of 1,500 meters, whereas a person can only see the same rabbit from 300 meters away. Schwartz calls for readers to extend this reasoning: "Measure (or estimate) 1,500 meters. What can you see from that distance?"

In what ways does *If You Hopped Like a Frog* meet the four criteria of effective math-related books?

Mathematical Integrity. If You Hopped Like a Frog reflects several of NCTM's Content Standards. The entire book illustrates the concept of ratio in a wide range of contexts, thus addressing the Algebra Standard. Measurement is reflected in many forms: linear, weight, area, volume, capacity, and time, with examples of both metric and customary systems. The Process Standards are evident as well. Schwartz's opening letter demonstrates the Problem-Solving Standard by opening a window into the way the problems emerged from a real-life context of observing frogs. His demonstration of curiosity, research, and perseverance helps "to promote the development of all students' dispositions to do mathematics" (NCTM 2000, p. 91). In the endnotes, readers are invited to pose and solve related problems. Consistent with the Communication, Representation, and Reasoning and Proof Standards, Schwartz explains his calculations through language, symbols, and drawings. Reflecting the Connections Standard, the book connects mathematics and science in meaningful ways. In addition, connections are made between mathematical topics, such as relating fractions to decimals.

The mathematical content is also presented in ways that are accessible to a wide range of readers. One of the easiest calculations

---

Math-Related Books Should Demonstrate:

1. Mathematical integrity
2. Potential for varied response
3. An aesthetic dimension
4. Racial, cultural, and gender inclusiveness

involves the snake. If a snake has a head measuring 1 inch across, it can swallow prey that measures 2 inches across. It follows that "If your head were 5 inches across from ear to ear and you swallowed like a snake, you could gulp down something 10 inches thick—like a telephone pole!" The eagle example is more complex and therefore presents a more sophisticated challenge for more experienced readers: it relates an example of density (number of cones contained per square millimeter of retina) in a context that involves distance (number of meters of visual acuity). From the very simple to the most challenging examples, Schwartz conveys an attitude that mathematics is intriguing, enjoyable, and satisfying. His description of his boyhood musings also serves as a powerful demonstration of entries that children might include in writers' notebooks (Fletcher 1996).

Potential for Varied Response. Schwartz's book meets this criterion in several ways. Since it naturally integrates mathematics and science, the book promotes varied response by inspiring readers to research other animals, study the nature of adaptation, observe animals closely, and design their own mathematical stories and informational texts. The book appeals to a wide range of ages, another aspect of varied response. One group of first-grade children explored how long their tongues would be if they were like a chameleon (1/2 body length). They cut pieces of adding machine tape as long as their bodies and then folded the tape in half to represent their "chameleon tongue" (Schwartz 2001). A sixth-grade class researched interesting attributes of other animals, applied Schwartz's strategies for comparison, and composed their own "if" stories and illustrations (Schwartz 2001).

> "You can almost divide the nonfiction [children] read into two categories: nonfiction that stuffs in facts, as if children were vases to be filled, and nonfiction that ignites the imagination, as if children were indeed fires to be lit."
>
> Source: Jo Carr, "Filling Vases, Lighting Fires," *Horn Book* 63 (November/December 1987): 710.

An Aesthetic Dimension. Both the text and the illustrations of *If You Hopped Like a Frog* tickle the imagination and inspire awe about the wonders of nature. Young readers better appreciate the activity of shrews, spiders, and other creatures through comparisons that relate directly to children's common experiences and interests, such as eating hamburgers and running on a football field. By addressing readers directly ("If you . . ."), Schwartz draws them directly into his hypothetical world. The exaggerated, humorous illustrations further accentuate these natural feats and add emotional appeal.

Racial, Cultural, and Gender Inclusiveness. Throughout the book, the accessibility of mathematical ideas reflects strong support for all learners. In addition, the illustrations promote positive gender attitudes. Both genders are dressed appropriately for physical activity and take active roles, such as lifting a car or flying like an eagle. The illustrations do, however, portray a majority of white children, and in one picture a mother wears a stereotypical apron. These reservations should be kept in mind and can be addressed when you're reading the book with children.

In summary, *If You Hopped Like a Frog* demonstrates value from both mathematical and language arts perspectives (see Figure 1.1). The book naturally embeds mathematical ideas in scientific settings. It appeals to readers through its humor and intriguing facts, and it invites readers to join the author in pursuing mathematical investigations and writing about them.

How Do Books Show Mathematical Integrity?

We now turn to a wide range of books to illustrate examples of both exemplary and poor quality for the criterion of mathematical integrity, since sometimes criteria become clearer through contrast. The following features further elaborate on this criterion:

- The mathematical components of the book are accurate.
- The mathematics reflects functional use in believable contexts.
- The ideas and concepts are accessible to the reader.

Mathematical Components Are Accurate

Using vocabulary appropriately is part of the Communication Standard. Although the focus of math-related books should not be on teaching vocabulary in a didactic way, when vocabulary is used accurately and in meaningful contexts, books can be powerful teaching tools about language as well as mathematical concepts. Concept books by Tana Hoban demonstrate appropriate use of mathematical vocabulary. Children who read her book *Cubes, Cones, Cylinders, and Spheres* (2000), for example, have the opportunity to become familiar and comfortable with mathematical terms. Throughout the book, photographs show these geometric solids in a variety of familiar contexts, such as traffic cones, bubbles, and smokestacks. Simple labeled sketches on the copyright page serve as a reference for the reader. Hoban's use of precise vocabulary rather than colloquial terms such as *box* or *ball,* or inaccurate labels such as *square* (for a three-dimensional *cube*) or *circle* (for *sphere* or *cylinder*), makes her books wise choices for the mathematics classroom.

uses correct vocab

On the other hand, an examination of *A Triangle for Adaora* (Onyefulu 2000) reveals mathematical inaccuracies. Although the book depicts cultural aspects of Nigeria through excellent photographs, the author confuses terminology for two- and three-dimensional figures. A three-dimensional conical hat, for example, is described with the two-dimensional term *triangle.* Furthermore, the story line seems forced and inauthentic. The main character, Adaora,

wrong vocab

Figure 1.1
An Illustration of the
Criteria in Use

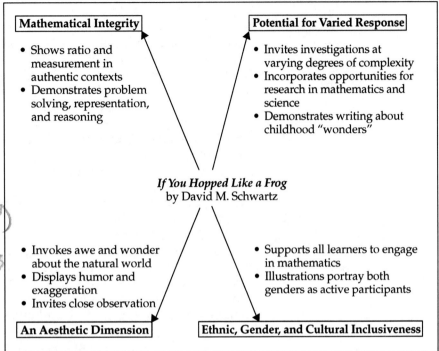

Mathematical Integrity

- Shows ratio and measurement in authentic contexts
- Demonstrates problem solving, representation, and reasoning

Potential for Varied Response

- Invites investigations at varying degrees of complexity
- Incorporates opportunities for research in mathematics and science
- Demonstrates writing about childhood "wonders"

If You Hopped Like a Frog
by David M. Schwartz

- Invokes awe and wonder about the natural world
- Displays humor and exaggeration
- Invites close observation

- Supports all learners to engage in mathematics
- Illustrations portray both genders as active participants

An Aesthetic Dimension

Ethnic, Gender, and Cultural Inclusiveness

refuses to eat a pawpaw because of its star shape, and her cousin embarks on a quest to appease her by "finding" a triangle. The problem of the story is merely a contrivance to assist the author in teaching geometric shapes.

Functional Use in Believable Contexts

Books that meet this criterion embed mathematical ideas in ways that are natural and useful. *Tiger Math: Learning to Graph from a Baby Tiger* (Nagda and Bickel 2000) incorporates two parallel texts. A wide variety of graphs on each left-hand page conveys mathematical information, while the right-hand pages relate events in narrative form.

In the narrative, T. J., the cub, faces danger when his mother dies. Veterinarians at the Denver Zoo must keep careful records to document the status of his health. Although T. J. accepts some food, his weight gain is slow. The accompanying line graph traces T. J.'s weight over time and compares it to his father's record of development. This graph demonstrates the functional uses of a line graph: to show change continuously over time and to compare and contrast sets of data. The book also includes several other graphical formats, such as pie charts, bar graphs, and pictographs. By comparing the various formats, learners can appreciate the benefits and limitations of each. Readers can, for example, compare the kinds of information that are represented on a pictograph and on a pie chart. One pictograph shows the population of several species of tigers and uses a scale of one picture to represent 500 tigers. Because only about 40 South China tigers exist in the world, it is too difficult to include this species on the pictograph, but the tigers are represented on the pie chart that follows. Readers see that a pie chart can show even small percentages, whereas pictographs might not be able to. It is these functional uses of data representation that lend mathematical integrity to the story (see Figure 1.2).

In contrast, we do not find that the portrayal of mathematics in *Inchworm and a Half* (Pinczes 2001) rings true. In this story, an inchworm uses its body to measure garden plants. When an item is too short to use a full body length, a smaller worm, representing a fraction, solves the dilemma. At one point, a "one-third"-inch worm comes to help. Do you find this fractional element a bit surprising in this context? We felt uncomfortable with the author's choice since rulers are *not* marked in thirds, but rather in fourths, eighths, and sixteenths. We would argue that this story does not portray the mathematics in a meaningful, authentic way.

[handwritten margin note: not a good book choice]

Accessibility of Ideas

Authors make mathematical ideas accessible through illustrations, analogies, real-life examples, and clear explanations. *On beyond a Million* (Schwartz 1999) and *Big Numbers* (Packard 2000) both use pictures, symbols, and narrative comparisons to describe large numbers. Think about these features as we examine how each book introduces the term *exponent*.

In Schwartz's (1999) book, Professor X explains:

> The little numbers are called exponents. An exponent tells you how many times to multiply a number by itself. (Unpaged)

A sidebar illustration on the same page shows the professor's dog, Y, in front of a chalkboard, on which is written:

> 10^2 is called ten to the second power.
> $10^2 = 10 \times 10 = 100$.
> $10^3 = 10 \times 10 \times 10 = 1,000$.

The dog Y is listening to a student, who asks, "So ten multiplied by itself three times is 10^3?"

Figure 1.2
Formats for Displaying Data

Which pet should our class get?

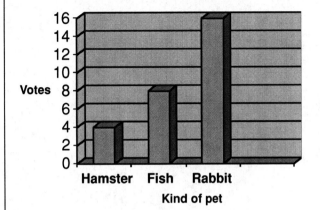

A bar graph is used mostly for discrete, or distinct, data. It can give a quick comparison of the categories of the data.

Which pet should our class get?

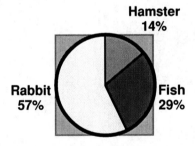

A pie chart shows parts of a whole (here, a whole class). The parts represent percentages of this whole (100 percent).

Temperatures from 6 a.m. to 10 a.m.

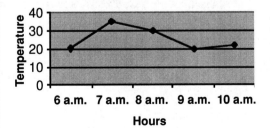

A line graph shows changes or variations over time. It represents continuous data, such as time, growth, or temperature.

In *Big Numbers*, Packard (2000) explains the same term, *exponent*, in a different way. On a page labeled "One Million," a text box reads:

> 10^6 with a little '⁶' is a short way to write 1,000,000. The little '⁶' is called an exponent. (Unpaged)

[handwritten margin note: doesn't vary in presenting Math info]

The text is accompanied by illustrated characters making comments in speech bubbles: "A million is a thousand thousands," and "Or one hundred times ten thousand." A second text box appears on the next page:

> If you ever want to write "ten million" fast, don't bother writing 1 and seven zeros. Just write 10^7. That's ten to the seventh power.

When we compared these two treatments of the same mathematical term, we concluded that a child reading Packard's book might learn only the mechanics of writing exponents. For several reasons, we believe that Schwartz makes the ideas more accessible to the reader. His definition of exponents includes the meaning behind the notation; that is, the exponent stands for the number of times a number is multiplied by itself. This information better helps readers generate other examples of exponents. Further, the expanded notation (e.g., $10 \times 10 \times 10$) pictured in the sidebar helps illustrate the relationship between the place value of the numbers and exponential notation. Thinking back to NCTM's Learning Principle, a guiding question might be, "Will children demonstrate understanding and connect and apply mathematical ideas after reading this book?"

[handwritten margin note: makes it more universal]

Illustrations play a key role in counting books and are therefore especially important to consider when evaluating books for accessibility of mathematical ideas. Illustrations in counting books should be clear and make counting easy. Well-designed counting books also have objects grouped in interesting ways that encourage children to count by sets or help them visualize number relationships. The sea life in *One Lonely Seahorse* (Freymann and Elffers, 2000), for example, is made up of easy-to-count, colorful shapes created from fruits and vegetables. On some pages, readers can count the animals in a variety of ways. Seven cranberry-bean eels, for instance, are arranged in two groups: four on one side, three on the other ($3 + 4 = 7$). There are ten pepper fish: four yellow, four red, and two green ($4 + 4 + 2$).

> **Pose Questions That Encourage Children to Count in Different Ways**
>
> a. Where shall we start counting?
>
> b. What is another way we can count?
>
> c. Why did we get the same answer?
>
> d. What groups of things do you see?

Accessibility of ideas can also be achieved through multiple forms of representation. Numbers in *Let's Count* (Hoban 1999) are represented by the numeral, the word, a photograph, and columns of dots that demonstrate place value for numbers greater than 10. One example shows 15 cookies arranged in a 3×5 array, the numeral 15, the word *fifteen,* and two columns of dots showing one ten and five ones.

In other books, the illustrations are not clear enough for children to count easily. *Ten Go Tango* (Dorros 2000) is a rollicking rhyme illustrated with fanciful watercolor drawings, but it is not as

> **Effective Illustrations for Beginning Counting Books**
> - Objects are not crowded on the page
> - Objects are about the same size
> - Objects to be counted are whole, not cut off
> - Objects are easy to distinguish from the background

helpful a book for children learning to count. Even though the largest group is only composed of 10 animals, some are difficult to count. Seven of the nine rhinos, for example, crowd one another across a double-page spread. One rhino has only one leg on the page, and two have parts of their heads off the page. For a small child learning to count, these kinds of illustrations are confusing. They make it difficult for the child to identify members of a set and to keep track of the items that have been counted.

How Do Books Invite Varied Response?

Good math-related books can invite varied response in many ways. They can include a range of mathematical ideas for children to investigate, discuss, and extend. They inspire children to collect mathematical musings and observations in their writer's notebooks and to use mathematical ideas in a variety of genres in writers' workshop. They sharpen a viewer's eye for specific details and relationships. They can also reflect an interdisciplinary perspective and thereby grant readers the opportunity to respond mathematically as well as historically, scientifically, and so on. As children engage in research, problem posing, and problem solving, they develop important attitudes and dispositions about the nature of mathematics and themselves as mathematicians. In order to evaluate a book's potential for varied response, a criterion to keep in mind is that the tone of the book should be invitational rather than didactic.

The Book Is Invitational

Grandpa's Quilt (Franco 1999) incorporates several mathematical ideas in a predictable story structure and can elicit a range of responses. In this humorous story, loving children try to solve a problem for their grandfather: his square coverlet, made of 36 quilt blocks in a 6 × 6 array, does not cover his feet. The children cut apart the quilt, rearrange it, and resew it as they strive to increase its length. Their first attempts, such as cutting the bottom row of 6 and sewing it to the top of the quilt, are unsuccessful. The story structure, the mathematical descriptions of the quilt, and the pictures all help readers predict and justify whether each attempt will succeed. The problem is solved when the children finally arrange the quilt blocks in a 4 × 9 rectangle. After reading the story, children might want to investigate numerical relationships, such as factors for 36 (the total number of quilt blocks) or the relationships between perimeter and area (the area of 36 blocks in the quilt remains constant, even though the perimeter changes as the rows are rearranged). Readers also

triggers further activities, discovering, hands-on experiments

might be inspired by the illustrations to use paper squares and triangles to create quilt block patterns, such as a rhombus or a star. The humorous story line might encourage children to dramatize the tale or to write and illustrate their own tales of exaggeration. Thus, the book demonstrates strong potential for promoting mathematical reasoning, representation, and communication and for developing language arts skills such as critical analysis, storytelling, and writing. This book is a valuable choice across a wide age range.

Books that are interdisciplinary in nature often invite varied response. *Ten Seeds* (Brown 2001), for example, invites both mathematical and scientific investigations. On the opening page, a child has just planted ten seeds, which are clearly illustrated and easy to count. An ant is carrying away one of the seeds. On each of the subsequent pages, a seed, or later a plant, succumbs to an unfortunate event, until just one plant remains. The book supports mathematical response by encouraging children to count backwards, to subtract successively by one, and to analyze the resulting mathematical pattern. There is also an opportunity for scientific response. The beautiful and scientifically detailed illustrations inspire readers to do some planting and observing themselves. Such a project could easily lead to data collection about germination success as well as growth over time. The book also embeds specific scientific vocabulary, such as *shoot* and *seedling*, in the delightful, poetic text. Finally, *Ten Seeds* engenders awe and wonder about the natural world. After nine of the original plants die, the one remaining plant replenishes the ten seeds, and the cycle can start again. What a miracle!

The Tone Is *Not* Didactic

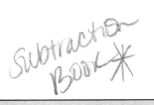

Subtraction Book ✱

An image that might come to mind as you read the word *didactic* in relation to literature is one of a controlled-vocabulary reader. We teachers have traditionally objected to forced, stilted stories and the way their narrow focus limits readers' responses. Here we are arguing that these considerations apply to the mathematical dimensions of books as well. *Subtraction Action* (Leedy 2000) portrays the operation of subtraction in only one way, but current research in mathematics advocates that children explore subtraction in a variety of contexts from the start of mathematics instruction (Kamii and Joseph 1989; Carpenter 1999; Trafton and Thiessen 1999). Let's take a close look at this book.

The story opens with a teacher introducing to her class a lesson in subtraction. The speech bubbles follow a traditional initiation-response-evaluation sequence of questioning:

> **Books That Portray Subtraction Situations**
>
> Comparison: *More, Fewer, Less* (Hoban 1998)
> Separating: *How Will We Get to the Beach?* (Luciani 2000)
> Part/Whole: *Ten Flashing Fireflies* (Sturges 1995)

> *Teacher:* What do these things have in common? [holding signs dealing with "less"]
>
> *Child:* They are all about **LESS**!
>
> *Teacher:* Right, Ginger, and to get less, we are going to **subtract**. (p. 4)

The teacher continues by posing a problem about the upcoming school fair. The class has 10 tickets to the fair. If they use 6 tickets, how many will be left over? The teacher leads the children through the conventional algorithm, which she illustrates on the board. She directs the children to begin by writing the "biggest number," then a minus sign for "take away," the equal sign, and finally the 4 to complete the equation.

$$
\begin{array}{r}
10 \\
-\ 6 \\
\hline
4
\end{array}
$$

She then quizzes the children: "Does anyone know what the answer is called?" (p. 5). The remainder of the book describes instructions for regrouping (represented by crossing out the numeral in the tens place) and for computing examples involving money. From time to time, the book directs specific questions to the reader, such as, "What is the difference between 10 and 5?" and supplies the answers on the last page. Like the students in the story, a child reading this book has little to contribute in response other than the correct answer.

You might be thinking, "How can a problem with one correct answer invite varied responses?" The key is not the answer itself but the processes that children use to arrive at the correct solution. Just as children draw on multiple strategies to make sense of print, so do they in mathematics. To find the difference between 10 and 6, some children might count up from 6 to 10 rather than subtract. Other children might build on their knowledge of 5 plus 5 and think, "I'll subtract 5 first ($10 - 5 = 5$) and then subtract one more ($5 - 1 = 4$)." Sharing these strategies would place emphasis on reasoning and number sense rather than on the manipulation of symbols. The long-term goal would be for children to choose efficient strategies for computation, which would vary depending on each problem's context.

We're also concerned with the attitudes and dispositions that might be conveyed through books such as *Subtraction Action.* Leedy's book implies that mathematical proficiency is synonymous with the memorization of rules, vocabulary, and procedures; that mathematics is learned by listening and following an expert rather than through collaboration and exploration; that mathematics is only palatable when it is "jazzed up" with cartoon characters or other "motivational" features; and that mathematics is not creative or rewarding. These are dangerous beliefs to perpetuate. This message is in contrast to NCTM's description of autonomous learners who are:

> [C]onfident in their ability to tackle difficult problems, eager to figure things out on their own, flexible in exploring mathematical ideas and trying alternative solution paths, and willing to persevere. Effective learners recognize the importance of reflecting on their thinking and learning from their mistakes. . . . When students work hard to solve a difficult problem or to understand a complex idea, they experience a very special feeling of accomplishment, which in turn leads to a willingness to continue and extend their engagement with mathematics. (2000, p. 21)

NCTM

The issue with Leedy's book, however, is *not* that it contains symbolic notation. Other books use conventional notation quite effectively. In *Bats on Parade* (Appelt 1999), for example, a marching band parades in a formation of successively large arrays (a single drum major-ette followed by four piccolo players in two rows and two columns, etc.). On each page, a mouse holds a banner that displays the corresponding equation, such as $3 \times 3 = 9$. At the same time, the illustrations of each group of instrumentalists provide geometric representations of this mathematical idea. Thus, the book opens avenues for further exploration of square numbers geometrically as well as numerically.

> **Questions to Consider When Evaluating a Book for Didactic Tone Might Include:**
>
> • Does the book direct a large number of single-answer questions to the reader?
>
> • Do frequent explanations or definitions interrupt the flow of the story in an awkward way?
>
> • Does the story seem contrived in order to fit an instructional purpose?
>
> • Does the author include prescriptive directions for parents to follow when reading the book with their children?
>
> • Is the book labeled with designations for a specific grade or sequential level?

We've summarized the "warning signs" of didactic books to consider in the sidebar on this page, and we conclude this discussion with a caveat: No book, no matter how invitational the tone, can guarantee the development of mathematical knowledge or healthy attitudes. How teachers, parents, and children interact with a book is the most critical consideration. We return to this idea in later chapters.

How Does a Book Incorporate an Aesthetic Dimension?

Books that have a didactic tone rarely have an aesthetic dimension. Since we have already discussed didactic books in depth, we devote this section to books of exemplary aesthetic quality.

We teachers all have favorite books that we read aloud every year, or that we return to again and again as demonstrations for writers' workshop. These books usually earn such high regard through their aesthetic appeal. When we focus our attention on math-related books, the aesthetic dimension also plays a key role. Good books appeal to the emotions and senses of the reader, provide a fresh perspective, and free the imagination. Here we discuss books that promote aesthetic response through:

- well-crafted language
- compelling illustrations, charts, diagrams, photographs, or other graphics
- a heightened awareness of form or design

Books that demonstrate well-crafted language and/or compelling illustrations and graphics: We discuss language and illustration together because ideally they complement and extend each other. Language can move readers with powerful imagery, rhythmic sounds, ironic twists, and striking comparisons. Well-chosen language can inspire laughter, tears, and wonder. In *Spots: Counting Creatures from Sky to Sea*, Carolyn Lesser (1999) portrays creatures with spotted fur or skin that live in the earth's ten biomes. The words that describe each animal, such as "[s]unning, slipping, diving" seals or "loping, gazing, nibbling" giraffes, roll from the tongue. Together with Laura Regan's stunning oil and gouache paintings, this text evokes wonder and respect for nature.

Aesthetic language and illustrations can be humorous as well. *Math Curse* (Scieszka 1995) is replete with wordplay, including puns and hyperbole. The math teacher's name is Mrs. Fibonacci; the science teacher is Mr. Newton. The narrator breaks the "curse" by adding 1/2 and 1/2 to make an escape "hole." The wide range of mathematical and verbal humor as well as the hilarious illustrations make this book accessible and entertaining to a range of readers.

When searching for good math-related literature, don't forget to include both humorous and serious poetry. By crafting language, "[p]oets help us see anew that which is a taken for granted part of our everyday world" (Bishop 2000). We suggest several individual poems as well as anthologies in Chapter 2.

Books that heighten awareness of form or design: Books can beckon readers to slow down, observe closely, and appreciate the world around them, the heavens, and the built environment. Such mathematical topics as spatial relations, weight, and geometric form are naturally embedded in *Nature Got There First* (Gates 1995). Gates reveals the engineering and design feats of plants and animals that have served as models for human invention, calling life "[a] natural experiment that began 3.5 billion years ago on Earth and is still in progress" (p. 7). In the living world, survival depends on meeting basic needs for food, shelter, and air, as well as protection from harm. Prairie dogs, for example, build above-ground ventilation towers that draw fresh air into their tunneled homes. Moving air above the towers lowers air pressure, and currents form, expelling stale air from the tunnels and letting fresh air in. Humans making tunnels, such as the rail tunnel under the English Channel, create similar ventilation systems, aided by fans, to keep air moving and fresh and to remove dangerous gases. Principles of design inspired by fish and other animals, such as the chambered nautilus, allow humans to sink in submarines or float with life preservers. The bases of 150-foot tropical rain forest trees need to be wide enough to balance their large crown of branches; architects use this principle to design buildings with buttresses. Gates helps readers appreciate not only the role of mathematics in the natural world but also the "cultural and intellectual achievements of humankind . . . including its aesthetic and even recreational aspects" (NCTM 2000, p. 4).

Without words, Arlene Alda opens readers' eyes to the beauty of both natural and manufactured objects in *Arlene Alda's 1 2 3* (1998) and *Arlene Alda's ABC* (1993). Each book is a collection of photographs that reveal the shapes of numerals and letters. The graceful curve of a swan's neck, mirrored by the surface of a pond, forms an exquisite 3, while a door handle and latch form a 5. Close-up photographs, such as a curly strand of hair for 6, encourage readers to notice small details.

Other books inspire awe of and appreciation for humanity. *One Hundred Is a Family* (Ryan 1994) broadens the definition of family to include neighborhoods and other large groups of people working together. Many of the best examples of books that honor humanity in aesthetic ways also promote ethnic and cultural equity, so we now turn to this last criterion of effective math-related books.

How Do Books Promote Gender, Ethnic, and Cultural Inclusiveness?

Math-related books for children should be free from bias. They should provide inspiration and role models, open doors for growth, and build appreciation for the historical and cultural contributions of all people. We have described this criterion in the following way: *The content, language, and illustrations promote racial, cultural, and gender equity.* Although much progress needs to be made in this area (Bishop 1994; Barrera 1997; Yokota 2001; Lehr 2001), there are some excellent books that meet this criterion. *The History of Counting* (Schmandt-Besserat 1999) is a particularly good example. The author, a prominent archaeologist, documents human inventiveness in developing mathematical tools across cultures and over time. She shows early forms of keeping records without numbers, such as notches etched on bones in the Middle East, and a system of body counting (pointing to different parts of the body to represent differ-

Author of *Arlene Alda's ABC*

Arlene Alda's
1 2 3

What Do *You* See?

ent numbers) that people in Papua New Guinea used. She also celebrates the invention of abstract systems of counting and, in particular, representations of zero. One strength of the book is her explanation for the diversity of number systems across time:

> Why did it take thousands and thousands of years to invent abstract numbers? Why weren't they invented sooner? It was not a question of intelligence: The size of your brain is the same as that of a child who lived fifty thousand years ago. Probably it was a matter of need.
> . . . It makes a lot of sense that counting became important when the

life of a community depended on knowing how many bags of grain to keep for planting the next harvest and how many animals would feed the village during the winter season. . . . But it was the tax system that had the biggest impact on counting. (pp. 20, 22)

Schmandt-Besserat truly appreciates mathematics as "one of the greatest cultural achievements of humankind" (NCTM 2000, p. 4) while honoring the ingenuity of diverse cultures across time and place. Her book encourages readers to do likewise.

Thirteen Moons on Turtle's Back: A Native American Year of Moons (Bruchac and London 1992) and *An Algonquian Year: The Year According to the Full Moon* (McCurdy 2000) both describe the measurement of time used by many Native American nations. Bruchac and London's book, however, is the stronger, while McCurdy's has the potential to perpetuate common stereotypes. *Thirteen Moons on Turtle's Back* opens as an Abenaki grandfather explains to his grandson that the pattern on the turtle's shell corresponds to the thirteen annual lunar cycles. Although many Native American peoples measure the year in this way, different nations have their own names and stories to describe each one. The authors carefully identify the origins of each of the thirteen captivating poems that follow. In the endnotes, readers learn that other Native nations in different climates divide the year in different ways, such as by dry times and times of rain, which further demonstrates diversity among Native peoples. From a mathematical perspective, this additional information helps to highlight that systems of measurement are arbitrary; like all mathematics, they reflect human invention.

In his introduction to *An Algonquian Year*, McCurdy describes the wide geographical range of Algonquian peoples and names several tribes. In the text, however, descriptions of seasonal activities, such as gathering maple sap, obscure tribal individuality, because not all tribes engage in that practice. Blending people together as if they were all the same reflects a biased view of culture (Slapin and Seale 1998). In addition, only twelve months are described in *An Algonquian Year*, but the lunar calendar consists of thirteen moons. Each page is labeled with the Gregorian term, such as January, as well as the Native label, such as Hard Times Moon, thus inaccurately implying a direct temporal correspondence. For these reasons, *Thirteen Moons on Turtle's Back* is the better choice from an equity perspective.

One Little, Two Little, Three Little Pilgrims (Hennessy 1999) reflects another poor treatment of Native Americans. Although Hennessy documents her research of Wampanoag life in the endnotes, she reverts to the historically demeaning practice of counting "Indians" (or here, Wampanoag) like objects (Slapin and Seale 1998). The greeting card–style illustrations perpetuate stereotypical caricatures, and the simplistic format conveys a romanticized harmony between Pilgrims and Wampanoag (Dorris 1978).

Another dimension of equity in math-related books is the portrayal of females. *One Grain of Rice* (Demi 1997), a folktale set in India, features a strong female protagonist. In this story, the greedy raja hoards almost all of the village's rice. The people face starvation until Rani takes clever and courageous action. She finds some grain that spilled from a basket during transit and, under the guise of obedience and respect, brings it to the raja. He offers her a reward, but instead Rani dupes him into an alternative plan: that the raja give her one grain of rice, to be doubled each day for thirty days. Rani's quick thinking and concern for equity save her fellow citizens. The story is valuable, then, not only for its positive gender role but also for its demonstration of political action on behalf of social justice. For these reasons, *One Grain of Rice* is a particularly good choice among the many books that involve a geometric progression.

Books such as *The Most Beautiful Roof in the World* (Lasky 1997) can serve as powerful demonstrations of career opportunities in the fields of mathematics and science for both girls and boys. In this book, Lasky chronicles the work of Meg Lowman, a rain forest scientist. Meg's interest in botany began very early; as a fifth grader, she won her state's science fair competition for her detailed study of flowers. Today Meg travels to rain forests around the world, where she focuses her inquiry on forest canopies. She must meet the physical challenges of climbing more than 100 feet above ground on specially designed apparatus and face the dangers of various poisonous creatures while gathering data. Much of her research focuses on the leaf-eating activity of insects, which involves precise measurement, data tabulation, and analysis. She examines the conditions of leaves over time, documenting rates of consumption. Meg's mathematical work has led her to generate several scientific hypotheses about the impact of leaf eating on the delicate balance of canopy health, and she has created experimental studies to gather additional data. At one point in the book, Meg invites her two sons to join her in collecting data about both plant and animal life, which further inspires young readers to investigate nature. Thus, this book is a valuable demonstration of career opportunities for both genders.

In a final word about equity, it is unfortunate that there are few examples of math-related books that reflect inclusion of people with disabilities. One book of note is *1 2 3 for You and Me* (Girnis 2001). Each page of this counting book consists of a photograph of a child wearing, playing with, or enjoying a variety of objects. The children represent many ethnicities; each has Down syndrome. The book helps to highlight the fact that this area of inclusiveness, like the others discussed in relation to this criterion, deserves increased attention in literature for children.

Looking Back and Looking Ahead

In this chapter, we have proposed criteria for teachers to use as they select math-related books for classroom use. These criteria incorporate important literary qualities, such as engaging story lines, well-crafted language, and illustrations that complement and extend the text. They also embody NCTM's *Principles and Standards for School Mathematics* (2000) in several ways. Good books demonstrate accurate mathematics used in functional, authentic contexts. They do not limit mathematical content to prescriptive procedures; instead, they open multiple avenues for all learners to explore ideas and to build understanding. Through these varied opportunities for investigation, these books support readers in developing healthy attitudes and dispositions about mathematical activity.

Since different books reflect each of the four criteria to varying degrees, it is teachers who must ultimately decide which books are best for their students. The overall guiding question should therefore be, "Is this book opening doors in the language arts and mathematical lives of *all* children in my classroom?" And, finally, it is important to remember that books reach their potential through the acts of reading and sharing. In the following chapters, we describe strategies that teachers have found to be helpful in using math-related books effectively with young students.

References

Books Cited That Meet the Criteria

Alda, Arlene. *Arlene Alda's ABC: What Do You See?* Berkeley, CA: Tricycle Press, 1993.

———. *Arlene Alda's 1 2 3: What Do You See?* Berkeley, CA: Tricycle Press, 1998.

Appelt, Kathi. *Bats on Parade.* Illus. Melissa Sweet. New York: Morrow, 1999.

Brown, Ruth. *Ten Seeds.* New York: Knopf, 2001.

Bruchac, Joseph, and Jonathan London. *Thirteen Moons on Turtle's Back: A Native American Year of Moons.* Illus. Thomas Locker. New York: Philomel, 1992.

Demi. *One Grain of Rice.* New York: Scholastic, 1997.

Franco, Betsy. *Grandpa's Quilt.* Illus. Linda A. Bild. New York: Children's Press, 1999.

Freymann, Saxton, and Joost Elffers. *One Lonely Seahorse.* New York: Arthur A. Levine Books, 2000.

Gates, Phil. *Nature Got There First: Inventions Inspired by Nature.* New York: Kingfisher, 1995.

Girnis, Margaret. *1 2 3 for You and Me.* Photos. Shirley Leamon Green. Morton Grove, IL: Albert Whitman, 2001.

Hoban, Tana. *Cubes, Cones, Cylinders, & Spheres.* New York: Greenwillow Books, 2000.

———. *Let's Count.* New York: Greenwillow Books, 1999.

———. *More, Fewer, Less.* New York: Greenwillow Books, 1998.

Lasky, Kathryn. *The Most Beautiful Roof in the World: Exploring the Rainforest Canopy.* Photos. Christopher G. Knight. San Diego: Harcourt Brace, 1997.

Lesser, Carolyn. *Spots: Counting Creatures from Sky to Sea.* Illus. Laura Regan. San Diego: Harcourt Brace, 1999.

Luciani, Brigitte. *How Will We Get to the Beach?* Illus. Eve Tharlet. New York: North-South Books, 2000.

Nagda, Ann Whitehead, and Cindy Bickel. *Tiger Math: Learning to Graph from a Baby Tiger.* New York: Henry Holt, 2000.

Nolan, Helen. *How Much, How Many, How Far, How Heavy, How Long, How Tall Is 1000?* Illus. Tracy Walker. Toronto: Kids Can Press, 1995.

Ryan, Pam Muñoz. *One Hundred Is a Family.* Illus. Benrei Huang. New York: Hyperion, 1994.

Schmandt-Besserat, Denise. *The History of Counting.* Illus. Michael Hays. New York: Morrow, 1999.

Schwartz, David M. *If You Hopped Like a Frog.* Illus. James Warhola. New York: Scholastic, 1999.

———. *On beyond a Million: An Amazing Math Journey.* Illus. Paul Meisel. New York: Random House, 1999.

Scieszka, Jon. *Math Curse.* Illus. Lane Smith. New York: Viking, 1995.

Smith, David J. *If the World Were a Village: A Book about the World's People.* Illus. Shelagh Armstrong. Toronto: Kids Can Press, 2002.

Sturges, Philemon. *Ten Flashing Fireflies.* Illus. Anna Vojtech. New York: North-South Books, 1995.

Wells, Robert E. *What's Faster Than a Speeding Cheetah?* Morton Grove, IL: lbert. Whitman, 1997.

Books Cited That Do *Not* Meet the Criteria

Dorros, Arthur. *Ten Go Tango.* Illus. Emily Arnold McCully. New York: HarperCollins, 2000.

Hennessy, B. G. *One Little, Two Little, Three Little Pilgrims.* Illus. Lynne Cravath. New York: Viking, 1999.

Leedy, Loreen. *Subtraction Action.* New York: Holiday House, 2000.

McCurdy, Michael. *An Algonquian Year: The Year According to the Full Moon.* Boston: Houghton Mifflin, 2000.

Onyefulu, Ifeoma. *A Triangle for Adaora: An African Book of Shapes.* New York: Dutton, 2000.

Packard, Edward. *Big Numbers: And Pictures That Show Just How Big They Are!* Illus. Salvatore Murdocca. Brookfield, CT: Millbrook Press, 2000.

Pinczes, Elinor J. *Inchworm and a Half.* Illus. Randall Enos. Boston: Houghton Mifflin, 2001.

Scholarly Works Cited

Austin, Patricia. "Math Books as Literature: Which Ones Measure Up?" *The New Advocate* 11 (1998): 119–33.

Barrera, Rosalinda B., Verlinda D. Thompson, and Mark Dressman, eds. *Kaleidoscope: A Multicultural Booklist for Grades K–8,* 2nd ed. Urbana, IL: National Council of Teachers of English, 1997.

Bishop, Rudine Sims, ed. *Kaleidoscope: A Multicultural Booklist for Grades K–8.* Urbana, IL: National Council of Teachers of English, 1994.

———. "Why Literature?" *The New Advocate* 13 (2000): 73–76.

Burns, Marilyn. *Math and Literature (K–3).* Sausalito, CA: Math Solutions Publications, 1992.

Carpenter, Tom, and Elizabeth Fennema. *Children's Mathematics: Cognitively Guided Instruction.* Portsmouth, NH: Heinemann, 1999.

Dorris, Michael. "Why I'm NOT Thankful for Thanksgiving." *Interracial Books for Children Bulletin* 9 (1978): 6–9.

Fletcher, Ralph. *A Writer's Notebook: Unlocking the Writer within You.* New York: Avon, 1996.

Kamii, Constance, with Linda Leslie Joseph. *Young Children Continue to Reinvent Arithmetic—2nd Grade: Implications of Piaget's Theory.* New York: Teachers College Press, 1989.

Lehr, Susan, ed. *Beauty, Brains, and Brawn: The Construction of Gender in Children's Literature.* Portsmouth, NH: Heinemann, 2001.

National Council of Teachers of Mathematics. *Curriculum and Evaluation Standards for School Mathematics.* Reston, VA: National Council of Teachers of Mathematics, 1989.

———. *Principles and Standards for School Mathematics.* Reston, VA: National Council of Teachers of Mathematics, 2000.

Schwartz, David M. "'We disagree with what you wrote': Challenging the Author and Other Delights." Paper presented at the Association of Mathematics Teachers of Connecticut Annual Conference, Cromwell, CT, March, 21, 2001.

Slapin, Beverly, and Doris Seale, eds. *Through Indian Eyes: The Native Experience in Books for Children.* Los Angeles: American Indian Studies Center, University of California, 1998.

Trafton, Paul R., and Diane Thiessen. *Learning through Problems: Number Sense and Computational Strategies.* Portsmouth, NH: Heinemann, 1999.

Whitin, David J., and Phyllis Whitin. "What Counts in Math-Related Books for Children." *Journal of Children's Literature* 27 (Spring 2001): 49–55.

Whitin, David J., and Sandra Wilde. *Read Any Good Math Lately? Children's Books for Mathematical Learning, K–6.* Portsmouth, NH: Heinemann, 1992.

Whitin, David J., and Sandra Wilde. *It's the Story That Counts: More Children's Books for Mathematical Learning, K–6.* Portsmouth, NH: Heinemann, 1995.

Yokota, Junko, ed. *Kaleidoscope: A Multicultural Booklist for Grades K–8,* 3rd ed. Urbana, IL: National Council of Teachers of English, 2001.

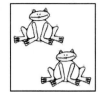

2

Books for a Wide Range of Ages

In Chapter 1, we identified "potential for varied response" as one of four criteria for selecting math-related literature for children. Some of the best books exemplifying this criterion are those that offer rich avenues for exploration to children of a wide age range. In this chapter, we examine closely three books that encompass many mathematical concepts and different literary genres. We listen in as K–6 teachers invite children's observations and comments about these books. We see how children engage in mathematical, language arts, and scientific experiences through reading and talking, and we suggest additional possibilities for you to explore with your own students. By vicariously joining these classrooms and examining these books, we hope to offer new perspectives for using old favorites as well as recently published books. We've included a collection of titles to consider; we trust that you will add others. A thumbnail sketch of the chapter includes:

- A brief discussion of the value of books for a wide age range
- A close look at the ways K–6 teachers and children have explored three exemplary books
- Poetry for all ages
- A reflective review of the classroom examples from the perspective of the mathematics and language arts Standards
- A collection of recommended titles for a wide age range

The Benefits of Exploring Books for a Wide Age Range

A primary reason we have chosen to share these particular books is to offer ideas to teachers of various grade levels. But we also believe that by grouping stories from different classrooms, we can offer an enriched perspective of the spiraling nature of conceptual understanding. The Standards for both mathematics and language arts emphasize revisiting key concepts in a variety of contexts with increasing sophistication over the years. Examining these classroom examples as a whole can open a window onto this process. What, for

focus on individual learning needs {

example, do young children's observations about symmetry tell us about their emerging understandings? In what ways are older children's explorations related to investigations in earlier years? Once aware of these links, how might teachers connect, revisit, challenge, or extend children's thinking? Thus, reading these anecdotes can serve as a vicarious cross-grade teachers' forum.

Of course, experienced teachers are well aware that even within a grade-level class, children are individuals, with a variety of interests and abilities, and many are at various points of learning English as a second language. A second benefit of exploring books for a wide age range, then, is the ability to entertain a range of curricular explorations around a book that can be tailored to particular classroom contexts. Knowing the range of possibilities helps teachers meet the needs of individual children, and the classroom examples highlight some of those possibilities.

We also preface the classroom stories with an overview of each book. Before reading the books with their students, the teachers whose classrooms are discussed in this chapter read and reread the books, examining them for literary themes, author's craft, and range and depth of mathematical content. Later they read the books aloud with their students and framed conversations around open-ended questions. The follow-up explorations grew out of many considerations: the children's observations and interests, interdisciplinary connections, curricular expectations, time, and availability of resources. Let's now turn to their experiences.

How Can I Judge If a Book Is Appropriate for a Wide Range of Ages?

1. Brainstorm the book's mathematical potential first. It is helpful to do this brainstorming with colleagues who teach at different grade levels to get a sense of the range and depth of the mathematical ideas.

2. Look for universal literary qualities, such as a sense of wonder and awe, or a playfulness with language, as well as broad human themes, such as greed, power, compassion.

Classroom Explorations of Three Exemplary Books

I Can Count the Petals of a Flower

Wahl, John, and Stacey Wahl. *I Can Count the Petals of a Flower.* Reston, VA: National Council of Teachers of Mathematics, 1976.

Although this book has been in print for many years (and still is), we wanted to feature it for two reasons. First, since it is published by NCTM and therefore not available in mainstream bookstores, many teachers are not familiar with it. Second, it offers a wonderful opportunity for children to connect numerous ideas in math, science, and language arts. This is a two-part counting book comprising close-up color photographs of flowers. The only words are the names of the flowers underneath each photograph. In the first section there is one flower per page: 1 petal of a lily, 2 petals of a crown of thorns, 3 petals of a snowdrop, and so on. In the next section, numbers 1, 2, and 3 all are shown through a single photograph (as before), but 4

begins to show factors for composite numbers. Here there are two photographs: 1 Chinese dogwood with 4 petals and also 2 crown-of-thorn flowers with 2 petals each. Number 6 is shown through three photographs: 1 yellow day lily (1 × 6), 2 painted trillium (2 × 3), and 3 crown of thorns (3 × 2) (see Figure 2.1).

Figure 2.1
Flower Petals Showing
Factors for 6:
$1 \times 6 = 6$; $2 \times 3 = 6$; $3 \times 2 = 6$

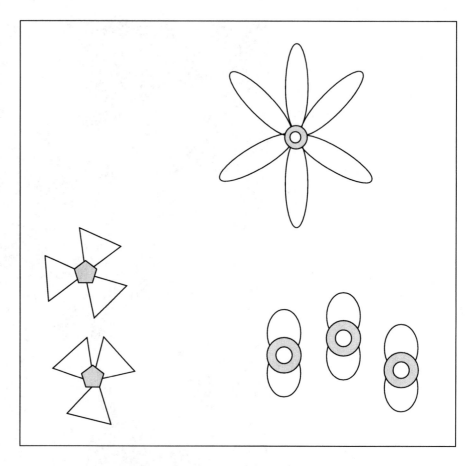

The book offers many mathematical and literary opportunities for exploration:

Mathematical Potential

- Highlights prime and composite numbers, factors, and multiples

- Integrates math and science

- Invites predicting of patterns

Language Arts Potential

- Demonstrates the craft of a visual text

- Evokes wonder; inspires questions for research

- Spurs interest in etymologies of flower names

As a way to demonstrate the many benefits of this text, we share examples from a variety of elementary classrooms. We have divided these examples into three categories in order to highlight the range of possibilities: making mathematical connections, examining an author's craft, and developing lines of research. Obviously, these categories are interwoven, but we separate them as a convenient organizing tool for the reader.

Making Mathematical Connections

When reading the second section of *I Can Count the Petals of a Flower*, where composite numbers are represented through several photographs, the children in many classrooms connected these pages to odd and even numbers:

> "I think the 2 petal flowers are going to come out again [predicting] because even numbers is something multiplied by 2." (grade 3)

Other Books That Invite Counting-On:

The Father Who Had 10 Children (Guettier 1999)

How Many Feet in the Bed? (Hamm 1991)

How Many, How Many, How Many (Walton 1993)

Only One (Harshman 1993)

Two Ways to Count to Ten (Dee 1988)

What Comes in 2's, 3's, and 4's? (Aker 1990)

> "There's been a crown of thorns on every other page. Do you know why? Because you can count by 2s evenly, and on the odd numbers you add only odd numbers, and the crown of thorns does not have an odd number of petals, so it can't be on those pages. So it's on every other page." (grade 4)

> "Almost all the odd numbers have just one photograph." (grade 2)

> "On the number pages 2, 4, 6, 8, 10, 12, and 14, the author counted by 2s. They all have the crown of thorns on it, and they counted by 2s." (grade 1)

The first-grade children then connected this counting by 2s in the book to the counting-on they had been doing on the 100 chart. In another second-grade classroom, a lively discussion about odd and even numbers arose when the children discussed the photographs for 9:

> *Child 1:* "If 9 is an odd number, then why does it have 3 groups? I think they made a mistake."

> *Child 2:* "Nope, they didn't make a mistake. Look, there are 9 petals there because 3 plus 3 plus 3 is 9."

> *Child 3:* "I guess some odd numbers you can put in groups, and there won't be 1 left over."

This discussion helped them refine the differences between odd numbers that have one photograph (primes) and those that have more than one photograph (composites).

The fourth graders cited earlier began to understand that odd composite numbers have only odd factors. They also connected this odd/even relationship to remainders and then to a distinction between multiplication and division:

> *Child 1:* "Even numbers have more pictures because you can show them in more ways. For 6 you have 3 flowers with 2 petals, and 2 flowers with 3 petals, and you don't have any remainders."

> *Child 2:* "This reminds me of division."

> *Child 3:* "It is, but it's a lot like multiplication."

> *Child 4:* "Well, they are just opposites of each other, so it's about both. It's like a fact family."

Dealing with remainders conjured up the association with division, and adding sets of petals reminded them of multiplication. Their connection is an apt one, since division involves two sets, like multiplication, but one set is unknown (e.g., how many sets of 2 are in 9?).

Just as this fourth-grade class examined the differences between these operations, a second-grade class debated the relationship between addition and multiplication:

Child 1: "I think there are more ways for 6, because 5 plus 1 is 6."

Child 2: "But then they wouldn't be the *same* flower. See, there's 2 flowers that are the same, and they each have 3 petals. But they are all the same flower."

Child 3: "Yeah, like for 7, if you had a 4 and a 3, or a 5 and a 2, they wouldn't be the same flower. If you try to make 7 with 2, you can't because when you look at the number line you can see that there's 1 left if you go counting by 2s, and the same thing happens with 3."

Other Books That Show Names for a Number in Addition:

Jelly Beans for Sale (McMillan 1996)

One Is a Snail, Ten Is a Crab (Sayre and Sayre 2003)

Ten Flashing Fireflies (Sturges 1995)

Ten Red Apples (Miller 2002)

These children were expressing the important difference between these two operations: addends in addition can be different amounts, whereas factors in multiplication are equal sets. Thus, children of various abilities can make connections to odd and even numbers with increasing levels of sophistication.

After reading this book, several classes wanted to represent more than 15 petals (the last number in the sequence). A third grader and a fifth grader worked together to find other possibilities. They used many of the flowers depicted in the book to express their solutions, such as:

18

1 flower with 18 petals (1×18)

2 tickseed with 9 petals each (2×9)

9 crown of thorns with 2 petals each (9×2)

3 yellow day lilies with 6 petals each (3×6)

6 wake-robins with 3 petals each (6×3)

19

1 flower with 19 petals (1×19)

A third-grade class also wanted to go beyond 15 but used sets of items other than flowers. One child used spiders, frogs, octopi, and octagons to show sets for 16 (see Figure 2.2).

In summary, this text provided the catalyst for some fruitful investigations related to odd, even, prime, and composite numbers, as well as to the relationships between various operations. But the author's crafting of the text was also an area of interest for many students.

Examining the Author's Craft   Children were intrigued with many aspects of the author's craft: the style and genre of the book, the ending, the pattern and variation of the text, and the relatively sparse format. In a first-grade classroom, the children were interested in how the author combined two styles

Figure 2.2
One Child's Extension of *I Can Count the Petals of a Flower*

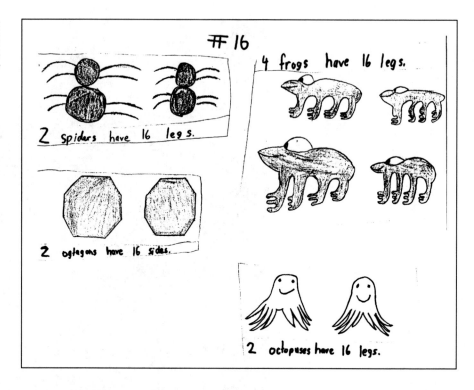

of books that the students were familiar with. As one child suggested, "This is a math and a science book. It's a math book because it starts at the number one and keeps counting higher and higher. And it's a science book because we see flowers."

Some fourth graders used some mathematical and scientific reasoning as they debated why the author concluded the book with the number 15. Was this a good decision?

> *Child 1:* "Well, it might be really hard to find flowers with all those petals."
>
> *Child 2:* "If they just stopped at 7, some people might not understand prime numbers. When you get to 9, you learn that all odd numbers aren't prime."
>
> *Child 3:* "We also learned that 13 was odd and prime, but 15 isn't. I think [ending at 15] is a good choice."
>
> *Child 4:* "Yeah, because maybe some people might think that after 10 there aren't any more prime numbers."

These children used their knowledge of prime and odd numbers to evaluate how the author constructed this text.

A class of sixth graders wondered how such a sparse text could generate so many questions: "I was surprised with how many things we found out because the book has no words [narrative text]. *Did the author do that on purpose?* There were lots of things to think about." This student's comment raised questions about the choices authors make. In this case, the author limits the number of things that readers pay attention to: photographs, labels, and numbers. The children noticed that by limiting what readers see, authors can sometimes prompt more wondering and speculating.

Third graders also discussed the pattern of the book. When the teacher began to show the second counting sequence, the children made some predictions:

> *Child 1:* "It's still going to count by 1s, but the flowers are going to be different."
>
> *Child 2:* "I think the numbers are going to count by 2s this time."
>
> *Child 3:* "I know the book is going to be different and not the same over and over again."
>
> *Child 4:* "Maybe the authors don't want us to focus on the counting this time, but they want us to focus on the flowers."

These children were highlighting an important aspect of an author's craft: variation. Authors do not keep repeating text features again and again, because they know they must hook the reader and maintain interest. Even predictable texts (such as this one) must break that pattern at some point to sustain interest and suspense. By examining this text, the children learned about the tension between predictability and variation.

Other Counting Alphabet Books:

The Icky Bug Counting Book (Pallotta 1992)

Mrs. McTats and Her Houseful of Cats (Capucilli 2001)

So Many Bunnies (Walton 1998)

26 Letters and 99 Cents (Hoban 1988)

Some second graders were intrigued with the genre the author selected. The counting book format reminded them of an alphabet book. One child in particular kept comparing the flowers to different letters of the alphabet, such as, "Hey, the snowdrop is an *S* word." For this reason, the teacher invited the students to create their own alphabet counting book.

The children used one set of objects at the top of each page to represent the letter and used multiple sets of flowers at the bottom to show the factors for the number (see Figure 2.3). As authors, they combined two organizational tools into one text.

Developing Lines of Research

The open-ended nature of *I Can Count the Petals of a Flower* opened many avenues for research. The second graders' alphabet counting book, for example, led to some unexpected research into language. One child decided to write her counting alphabet in Spanish, but when she began to look for a *w* word in the Spanish dictionary, she found none! She shared her discovery with the rest of the class.

Figure 2.3
Page from Students'
Alphabet Counting Book

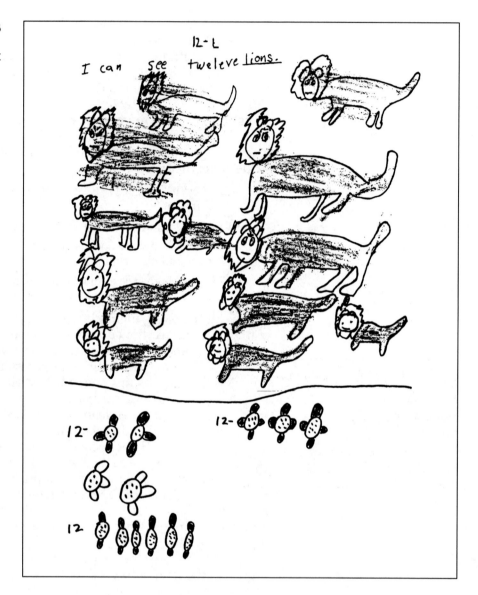

Many were surprised and checked the dictionary themselves to be sure this claim was correct. They became intrigued with how different languages have different sounds and alphabets. The students were coming to understand that alphabets are human inventions, not absolutes. They now realized that there are many alphabets, and they appreciated this diversity, wanting to know more about the Spanish language.

Another aspect of language that fascinated many children was the names of the flowers. As they read the labels, they proposed their own hypotheses about the origin of these names:

> "I wonder how the bloodroot flower got its name. Maybe because the water travels through the stem to all parts of the flower. The stem is like a highway. Everything travels through the stem like veins and blood in our body. (grade 4)

> "I think maybe the bloodroot has thorns, and if you touch it you can get pinched and bleed. Or maybe it has red roots." (grade 2)

> "The windflower reminds me of a pinwheel, or windmill. That's probably why they named it that way." (grade 5)

> "The star flower looks very similar to a star. It even has a twinkle to it." (grade 5)

Again, follow-up research using the dictionary, Internet, and other nonfiction resources helped the children learn more about these flower names. They found, for instance, that the bloodroot flower does in fact have a fleshy, red root and red sap. So the children's hypotheses were quite well founded!

A sixth-grade class raised a variety of questions that led to some scientific research:

> *Child 1:* "This book has a lot of white, yellow, and orange. Are these common colors for the petals?"

> *Child 2:* "Sixteen has a pink dogwood. There are Chinese dogwoods and pink dogwoods. I wonder if there are any other dogwoods."

> *Child 3:* "Are there any flowers you can eat?"

> *Child 4:* "Why do petals fall off?"

> *Child 5:* "What's the largest number of petals on a flower? I think a rose has a lot of petals. How come there were no roses in this book?"

These sixth graders raised so many questions for research that their teacher arranged a visit to the school greenhouse to find out more (Ventura 2001). Although horticulture was a seventh- and eighth-grade elective only, the children received special permission to visit the greenhouse. They learned how brightly colored petals with darker centers attract insects seeking nectar and that these insects help pollinate the flowers. They learned that once a flower is pollinated, its petals shrivel and fall off. The book and this visit prompted them to do even further research. Some students researched edible flowers. Others labeled the parts of flowers and described their function. A few students researched roses. Several created a computer-generated graph comparing different flowers and their number of petals. Thus, the book inspired a wide range of research interests.

Other Books That Integrate Mathematics and Science:

The Big Bug Book (Facklam 1994)

If You Hopped Like a Frog (Schwartz 1999)

Lifetimes (Rice 1997)

The Math Book for Girls and Other Beings Who Count (Wyatt 2000)

Spots: Counting Creatures from Sky to Sea (Lesser 1999)

Tiger Math: Learning to Graph from a Baby Tiger (Nagda and Bickel 2000)

What's Faster Than a Speeding Cheetah? (Wells 1997)

In other classes, students used their scientific research to create their own books. A class of fourth graders used the idea of multiples but applied it to animals. They worked in pairs to find interesting statistics about animals that related to their number. One pair found interesting facts related to 8: a beetle has 8 legs, a bullfrog can be about 8 inches long, and a skate can be as much as 8 feet across (see Figure 2.4). They used the mathematical perspective of the book but changed its emphasis to animals.

A first-grade class became interested in the counting-on aspect of the book because they had been counting-on by 2s, 5s, and 10s on their 100-square chart. Their teacher invited them to research their own flowers and then construct their own counting book. They worked in groups of two or three, eagerly searching through several nonfiction resources to find different flowers for each number. They realized that if they could find a 2-petal flower they could use it to make other even numbers. One group found a sego lily of 3 petals to represent 9, while another group decided to use two addends to represent the prime numbers. For instance, they used a 4-petal evening primrose and a 3-petal spiderwort to represent 7 (see Figure 2.5). The children loved learning the names of new flowers, and they were able to use their counting-on skills in a new context.

In summary, *I Can Count the Petals of a Flower* offers many learning opportunities for a wide range of children. Examples of students' responses include mathematical investigations into odd and even and prime and composite numbers, as well as discussions about the distinctions between addition and multiplication and between multiplication and division. Children examined different aspects of the author's craft, such as why the sequence ended with number 15, how such a sparse text generated so much discussion, and how the author varied a predictable text structure to keep the attention of readers. They conducted investigations into other kinds of flowers, the parts of flowers, the average number of petals of flowers, and the etymologies of flower names. Clearly, this book encouraged a wealth of response by many children.

Two Greedy Bears

Ginsburg, Mirra, adapt. *Two Greedy Bears*. Illus. Jose Aruego and Ariane Dewey. New York: Aladdin, 1998.

In this amusing retelling of a Hungarian folktale, two bears argue over a large chunk of cheese. A clever fox, offering to help them, breaks the cheese unevenly. When the bears protest, the fox eats just enough of the larger portion to make the pieces unequal once more, and the cycle is repeated. In the end, the two bears sadly find that although they now have equal shares of the cheese, those shares are merely the size of crumbs.

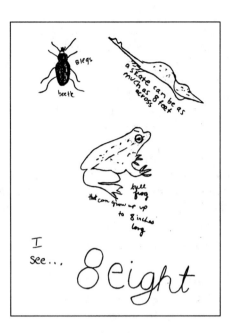

We have selected this tale as a fine example of a book that is appropriate for a wide age of readers for several reasons:

Mathematical Potential	**Language Arts Potential**
• Provides a meaningful context for fractions	• Conveys widely accessible themes, such as consequences of greed and brains over brawn
• Exemplifies several concepts, such as equivalence, ratio, congruence, and symmetry	• Connects with other trickster tales and "sly fox" characters

We take a look at how some K–5 teachers and students discussed and explored these potentials, with particular attention to mathematical content. We have grouped brief anecdotes under the two most direct mathematical connections to the story: equivalence and ratio. The entire problem of the story, not being able to divide the cheese equally, concerns equivalence (in this case, equal-size volumes). The story's ironic conclusion, when the bears do get equal but tiny shares, highlights the idea of ratio (the relationship of one to two parts, 1:2). One-half (or any ratio) is a constant relationship, not a constant amount; 1/2 of the large chunk of cheese is much different from 1/2 of a little crumb. We have created these two categories—equivalence and ratio—for the convenience of grouping the classroom examples and activities. In reality, these mathematical ideas are always interrelated.

Equivalence, Congruence, and Symmetry

In our classroom examples, many children demonstrated their understanding of equivalence when they discussed the story's problem. One kindergartner used the word *equal* in an inventive way to explain her interpretation of the bears' dilemma: "It's not fair, because the fox ate the big cheese. She ate it all; they [the bears] didn't know how to <u>equal half</u> it." In another case, a first grader explained, "The cheese was broke into two parts, but one piece was bigger than the other. That's not <u>one-half</u>." These kinds of comments demonstrate an understanding of the mathematical definition of one-half, particularly that halves must be equal amounts.

Jackie Dominguez asked her second graders to consider how the bears might have solved the problem for themselves. Some of their suggestions included:

> *Child 1:* "Put one piece on top of the other to see if they are the same."
>
> *Child 2:* "Cut the cheese in a lot of pieces and give the same number to each."
>
> *Child 3:* "Use a ruler to measure. If the two pieces are the same inches, then they are halves."
>
> *Child 4:* "You can put the pieces in that machine they have at the deli to see how many pounds they weigh, and if they weigh the same pounds then they are halves."

Through this discussion, the children considered a wide range of contexts for fractions as well as appropriate tools and strategies to use in these contexts. Matching the pieces of cheese involves congruence. Cutting the cheese into pieces and counting them shows a fractional part of a set (1/2 the total number of pieces). The last two children demonstrated that length and mass can be divided into fractional parts and that there are specific tools to use in each of those contexts. Following this discussion, Jackie asked the children to write and draw about the story in two ways. First they explained their solutions to the bears' dilemma. Figure 2.6 shows the proposed solution of dividing by weight at the deli (obviously influenced by the child's experience!). The children also created their own "equal share" stories. Figure 2.7 demonstrates two boys' application of fractions as part of a set. First the story characters try to sort a bag of M&M's by color, but the two resulting sets are not equal in number. They then solve their problem by counting the total number of M&M's and dividing that sum in two parts. Thus, their story demonstrated the boys' appropriate strategy of counting to determine half of a set.

In other classes, the follow-up discussions led to the topic of two-dimensional shapes and symmetry. While the class was talking about alternative solutions to the bears' problem, one kindergartner commented, "You have to fold it and cut it in the middle. That's

Figure 2.6
One Solution to the Problem
of One-Half

Figure 2.7
A Storytelling Solution to the
Problem of Equal Shares

equal sides" (two matching halves). Finding a line of symmetry was also discussed in Jena Napoli's fourth-grade classroom. These children explored how the shape of the object determined both the number of lines of symmetry as well as the number of solutions for obtaining equal halves. Figure 2.8 shows how one child showed that, unlike a circle, a triangular slice of pizza has only one line of symmetry.

Some upper grade children (fourth and fifth grades) explored the relationships between congruence, symmetry, and equivalence using area models for fractions. Are all symmetrical shapes equivalent? Are all equivalent amounts congruent? Walter Stark's fourth graders explored these ideas by representing 1/2 of the area of 4 × 3 grids (with areas of 12 square units). Shading 6 of them, no matter what the arrangement, resulted in shading in 1/2 of the total area. Thus, the students demonstrated that it is possible to have equivalent amounts that are not congruent in an area model. Figure 2.9 illustrates some of these solutions.

Exploring Fractions through a Set Model

The part-to-whole relationship in a fraction can be represented as a set model. A set of objects is subdivided into smaller groups of equal size. These books show this set model:

Five Creatures (Jenkins 2001): What are different ways to classify the people and animals in your family?

How Hungry Are You? (Napoli and Tchen 2001): In what different ways can friends share a set of cookies?

One of Three (Johnson 1991): How would you describe the different sets in your family?

Marianne Fuscaldo's first graders related their own "equal shares" experiences after hearing *Two Greedy Bears*. Most of their stories involved food, so Marianne designed a follow-up activity that built on their food stories. She wanted the children to consider fractions of a set, with both an odd and an even number of members. She designed a worksheet labeled "4 cupcakes" on one side and "5 cupcakes" on the other. She left the rest of the paper blank and invited the children to show their solutions for sharing each of these quantities equally, using pictures, numbers, and words. In this way, the children could make sense of the problem themselves, and they could represent their understanding in several ways. Figure 2.10 shows Eric's solution to the problem. For 4, he drew the cupcakes in 2 sets and noted the equivalence in the number sentence 2 + 2 = 4. With 5, he wrote, "I have 5 cupcakes. I take 2 and she takes 2 = 4. But there's 1 left. I will cut it in half. I take 1. She takes 1." His number sentence, 2 + 2 = 4 + 1 = 5, was his way of showing numerically this sequence of events, first dividing the set of 5 into 2 sets of 2, and then dealing with the remaining 1 cupcake, thus accounting for the total of 5 cupcakes (4 + 1 = 5). Grounding the problem in a familiar context enabled Eric and his classmates to solve and represent this complex example.

Finally, some follow-up discussions to *Two Greedy Bears* highlighted the language of mathematics. In one fifth-grade class, children discussed personal examples for 1/2. When one child contrib-

Figure 2.8
The Triangular Slice of Pizza
Has Only One Line of
Symmetry

Figure 2.9
Are Equivalent Areas Always
Congruent?

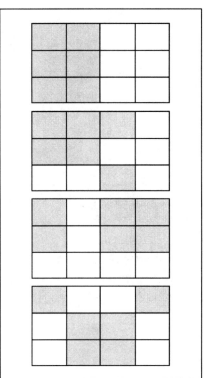

Figure 2.10
Eric's Solution to Equal
Shares

uted the context of "one-half of your homework," they realized that one-half can be an ambiguous term. A classmate objected, arguing that a person might have both spelling and mathematics homework. The mathematics might take longer than the spelling, so doing one of the two subjects would not divide the total amount of homework *time* in half. Deciding which attributes of a set "matter" in a given problem is an important dimension of problem solving, and these fifth graders were grappling with that very issue. A different problem with language arose in a fourth-grade class. One student remarked, "Sometimes you say one-half, but you don't mean it." Soon

> **Colloquial Uses for the Phrase "One-Half":**
> - I'm half asleep.
> - He was only half listening.
> - I've about half finished this job.
> - I don't have half a chance to win the contest.

the children were involved in a discussion that distinguished the figurative uses of one-half (e.g., "half-heartedly") from its precise use in mathematics. This too is an important issue to consider in developing an understanding of mathematical vocabulary (Rubenstein 2000).

A third exploration of the language of one-half occurred in Maria Kontaroudis' fourth-grade class. These children had recently read *Math Curse* (Scieszka 1995). After reading *Two Greedy Bears,* Maria asked, "What in our room shows one-half?" As their list grew, a few children asked if they could make books like *Math Curse* but based on the concept of one-half. Maria readily agreed. Creating their products enabled the children to explore the range of applications of one-half in Scieszka's playful, exaggerated style (see Figure 2.11).

These various examples demonstrate that equivalence is a multilayered concept. Children develop their understanding of equivalence by encountering it in different contexts and connecting it to different concepts, such as time, number, area, and symmetry. These examples from many grade levels give us a glimpse of some possibilities for exploration.

Ratio   In the context of fractions, ratio shows a relationship between the part and the whole. The size or quantity of the part varies with the size of the whole. In order to understand ratio, one must be able to think of two related numbers at the same time. *Two Greedy Bears* provides a meaningful context for this concept for even very young readers. Listening closely to their spontaneous comments helps teachers identify the students' level of understanding. One kindergartner, for example, explained, "The little crumbs weren't fair. They wanted big equal pieces." Older children are often able to express the same idea of ratio but in more depth. A fourth grader remarked, "There are all kinds of halves." "What does that mean?" probed the teacher. He continued, "No matter how big or small the piece, there is always a way of cutting something into equal pieces." His expla-

Figure 2.11. A Story of Halves

nation broadens the idea of ratio from the immediate context of the story to a generalization.

Ratio became an issue for discussion when a group of fifth graders considered how the bears might have made sure that their portions were equal. One child used her hand as an example, holding up her thumb, pointer, and 1/2 of her middle finger as one part and her pinky, ring, and 1/2 of her middle finger as the other part. Her teacher extended this idea: "Suppose your fingers were chocolate fingers and you could eat them. Which half of them would you rather eat if you wanted more, or are they both equal?" This example raised the issue that 1/2 of the number of fingers might not be the same as 1/2 of a specific mass. A lively discussion ensued, comparing the circumference of one's thumb and the length of one's pinky. The conversation led quite naturally to the topic of tools that would help verify their hypotheses, such as a scale to weigh the "chocolate fingers."

Other classes investigated another idea that relates to ratio: the inverse relationship between the number of pieces and the size of an individual piece. (Here again the children used an area model of fractions rather than volume.) This relationship can be demonstrated by a simple paper-folding experience that some fourth graders investigated. They took a sheet of paper and folded it in half, then half again, and again, and again. After each fold, the number of pieces doubled, and the size of each piece was halved. When the paper is folded in half, for example, there are 2 pieces, then four-fourths, eight-eighths, etc. (see Figure 2.12). Exploring this relationship addresses a common source of confusion about fractions: that in representing fractions, the larger the denominator, the smaller the piece.

In a fifth-grade class, a similar conversation about successive halving clarified the students' understanding of the meaning of multiplying fractions. These children enacted successive halving with a deck of cards. (Their teacher, Michael Beinert, allowed the children to cut up the cards when necessary to demonstrate the point.) They recorded the progression numerically on the board, starting with the full deck of 52 cards: 52, 26, 13, 6 1/2, 3 1/4, 1 5/8, 13/16, 13/32, 13/64. The children studied this record and then described in writing any patterns they saw. Several children described how the denominator always "doubled' when calculating half of the

---

Using 1/2 as a Benchmark for Comparing Fractions

Children can use the benchmark of 1/2 as a strategy for comparing fractions. In many instances, they can use reasoning to make this comparison rather than converting to common denominators.

Which is larger:

3/8 or 5/9? (3/8 is 1/8 less than 1/2 and 5/9 is 1/9 more than 1/2)

2/5 or 4/6? (2/5 is less than 1/2 and 4/6 is 1/6 greater than 1/2)

2/4 or 5/12? (2/4 equals 1/2 and 5/12 is 1/12 less than 1/2)

Source: John A. Van de Walle, *Elementary and Middle School Mathematics: Teaching Developmentally.* New York: Longman, 2001.

Figure 2.12
A Paper-Folding
Demonstration of Fractions

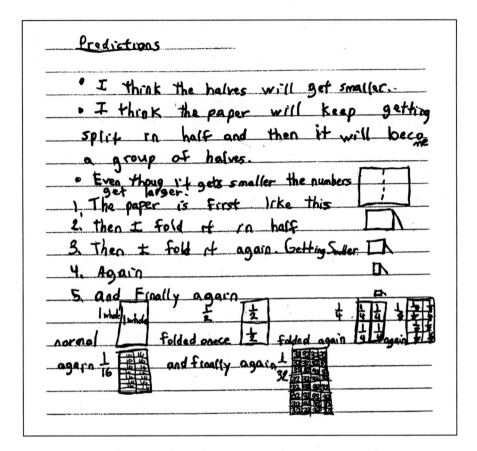

preceding fraction. One student explained that one-half is "dividing by two," while another called it "multiplying by one-half." Through exploring successive halving with a physical model (cards), recording the process numerically, and formulating a generalized description, these children clarified another common source of confusion regarding fractions: that when multiplying fractions, fractional parts are divided into smaller pieces (1 5/8 > 13/16 > 13/32). They also saw that the product is always smaller than either one of the factors when both factors are less than 1 (1/2 × 1/4 = 1/8).

In reflecting on these varied classroom examples, it is interesting to note that although the explorations became more sophisticated with the age and experience of the children, they all related to the same conceptual topic of ratio. Indeed, introducing the topic of ratio to young children lays a firm conceptual foundation that can be built on in later grades. For older children, exploring the topic of ratio through a story can create a shared context for learners of all abilities. *Two Greedy Bears* is an example of a book with this kind of potential. Appendix A offers additional explorations with one-half and other fractions.

Literary Explorations

Thus far we have focused mostly on the mathematical potentials embedded in the story of *Two Greedy Bears.* Before leaving our discussion of the book, we'd like to mention briefly other literary potentials in addition to the investigations of figurative language (expressions using one-half) mentioned earlier. The children in the classes described here analyzed the characters of the bears and the fox, proposed alternative endings, and explained their interpretations of the theme of the story. Some of the comments about the characters and theme are particularly interesting:

> **Other Math-Related Folktales:**
>
> *The Old Man's Mitten* (Pollock 1994)
> *One Grain of Rice* (Demi 1997)
> *Two of Everything* (Hong 1992)
> *Two Ways to Count to Ten* (Dee 1988)

- "When people fight over something, they are being greedy." (grade 1)
- "The bears wanted to be better than each other instead of even with each other." (grade 5)
- "The bears got what they deserved; if they weren't as greedy, they would have realized what the fox was doing and stopped the fox." (grade 4)
- "The book taught us a lesson. We should accept everything we have and not ask for more." (grade 4)

These comments suggest additional avenues for reading (e.g., finding other stories and poems with similar themes), writing (e.g., personal or fictional accounts with similar themes), and dramatization. Like the mathematical ideas, the literary themes are ones that recur in many language arts contexts and therefore cross a wide age range.

So Many Circles, So Many Squares

Hoban, Tana. *So Many Circles, So Many Squares.* New York: Greenwillow Books, 1998.

In this wordless picture book, Tana Hoban uses color photographs to invite readers to look closely at their world. Images include tessellations of shapes, such as the cobblestones on an old street and the grating on heating ducts. The author shows these shapes in different spatial orientations, such as the angled perspective of a street drain, and depicts three-dimensional shapes, such as grapes, radishes, and cardboard boxes. She also depicts the interplay between two- and three-dimensional shapes, such as the circular ring of a cylindrical tree trunk or the square ends of a rectangular cement prism. Readers can distinguish between the repetition of shapes created for aesthetic reasons (clothing) and those devised for functional reasons (stacking plates in a dishwasher). Interesting juxtapositions of photographs on double-page spreads include the wheels of a car and the tires of bicycles.

What makes this book appropriate for a wide range of age/ability levels? Some of its strengths include:

Mathematical Potential

- Shows a variety of contexts for shape
- Portrays a functional use of mathematics
- Invites connections between math concepts, such as symmetry, congruence, and area

Language Arts Potential

- Provides unique visual perspectives
- Highlights intriguing juxtapositions of photographs
- Offers an open-ended format

Teachers often use Hoban's books to help young children learn to identify basic shapes. They invite their students to find other examples of shapes in their environments and to create class books of photographs or drawings. An example of this kind of activity is described in Chapter 4.

You might be wondering how a concept book can be appropriate for upper elementary school children. As the children in this section demonstrate, looking closely is an appealing challenge for all ages. The key point is that these teachers framed the conversations in open-ended ways. Instead of asking, for instance, "Who can find a circle on this page?," these teachers asked such questions as, "Who would like to say something about this page?" With this kind of invitation, the children expressed a variety of ideas about geometry. Tana Hoban's books do not magically spark open-ended discussions. Rather, teachers who frame the discussion in exploratory ways really make the difference (Whitin and Whitin 2000).

A group of K–5 teachers taking a graduate mathematics class examined this book with their students and recorded the students' comments. Here we cite some of those comments, discuss the mathematical ideas embedded in them, and then suggest some activities that build on these observations and extend the mathematical thinking. We have grouped the children's comments/extensions under five categories: (1) investigating transformations of shapes; (2) making connections between two- and three-dimensional shapes; (3) inquiring into mathematical vocabulary; (4) examining the symmetry of regular polygons; and (5) exploring the area of irregular shapes.

Strategies for Sharing Picture Books with Older Students:

1. Be honest; tell them that the book might seem to be for younger children.

2. Assure them that they too can be challenged by the ideas in the book.

3. Pose open-ended questions for response, such as "Who would like to say something about this page? What do you notice or find interesting?"

4. Plan extension activities that build on the children's observations.

Figure 2.13
Stretching Squares into
Parallelograms

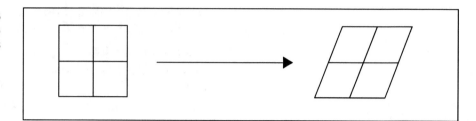

Investigating
Transformations
of Shapes

So Many Circles, So Many Squares can provide a useful starting point for children to discuss mathematical ideas in their own language. Often children do not know the conventional mathematical terminology for shapes and so they invent their own ways to describe what they see. It is important for teachers to encourage this language because children often highlight important attributes of shapes in this way. A third grader, for example, commented on a photograph of some netting, portions of which were squares while other sections were stretched into rhombi. He said, "The net is made up of all squares, even though some are pulled apart. If you stretched them back, they would be squares again." A classmate called the parallelograms "slanted rectangles." One kindergartner called these rhombi "lopsided squares" (see Figure 2.13).

Teachers can capitalize on such observations with follow-up explorations. A geoboard, for instance, is an excellent tool children can use to investigate these relationships, especially because it reenacts the photograph of the netting. Children can use rubber bands on the geoboard to stretch one shape into another. What happens to the area of a rectangle, for instance, when it is stretched into a parallelogram? What happens to the area of a square when it is stretched into a rhombus? Older children can determine that the areas remain the same and make a generalization about the area of any parallelogram: $A = L \times W$. Appendix B explains this activity in more detail.

Making Connections
between Two- and
Three-Dimensional
Shapes

Several third-grade children described three-dimensional shapes in interesting ways. One child called a cube "a puffed-up square," and another compared circles to ovals: "There are two kinds of circles: regular circles and ovals. Ovals are stretched-out circles. They're like smushed-out circles." This description of circles caused another child to remark that a cone has "a pointy top, a circle at the bottom, and it curls all around." As mentioned earlier, it is important for children to describe shapes in their own language before being introduced to mathematical terminology because their comments highlight significant attributes of those shapes. Recognizing the flat face of cubes and the circular base of cones is a noteworthy distinction to make. The

Figure 2.14
Shapes Found inside a
Ventilation Tube

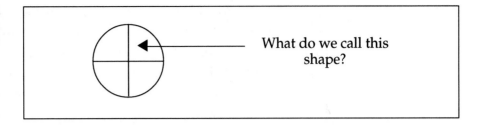

What do we call this
shape?

next step is for children to refine their initial descriptions by comparing these shapes to other shapes. Children might, for instance, compare a cone to other solid shapes: Can they find other shapes that have a pointy top (a pyramid), that have a circle on the bottom (a cylinder), or that curve all around (a sphere)? How are these shapes different? How are they the same? Children might compare a cube in the same way—e.g., How many of these other blocks have a square face? How many have more than two square faces? How many have rectangular faces? Triangular faces? Which have some of each? This kind of comparing and contrasting helps learners modify their attributes of shapes and make their descriptions more precise (Whitin and Cox 2003).

An excellent activity for comparing squares to cubes is known as pentominoes (Golomb 1965; Walter 1970). In this activity, children fold paper patterns of squares into boxes. Children can see how flat patterns of squares (known as nets) can "puff themselves up" into cubes. See Appendix C for further details about this investigation.

Inquiring into Mathematical Vocabulary

A fifth-grade class was interested in the shapes inside some ventilation tubes that are shown in *So Many Circles, So Many Squares.* Figure 2.14 provides a sketch of these shapes. The students began to debate whether these shapes were triangles or squares.

> *Child 1:* "Only half is a square."
>
> *Child 2:* "It's not a square because the edges are curved."
>
> *Child 3:* "I think this shape should be called a 'squircle' because it's half of a circle and half of a square."

Using what she knew about squares and circles, this last child invented the word *squircle* to describe this particular shape. This kind of language play is important because once children view themselves as inventors of words, they find it interesting to learn about the etymologies of other words. In this case, the word *circle* comes from the Greek word meaning "ring." The word *square* comes from the Latin meaning "four" *(quattuor)* or "to make square." Thus, a squircle partly looks like a ring and suggests four sides. Here is a list of some other geometry terms and their etymologies (Rubenstein 2000):

Mathematical Term	Etymology
Perimeter	*peri* = around, *meter* = measure
Parallel	*para* = alongside
Radius	*radius* = ray (e.g., a ray of light shining from a point)
Diameter	*dia* = across or through, *meter* = measure
Diagonal	*dia* = across or through, *gon* = angle
Polygon	*poly* = many, *gon* = angle
Circumference	*circum* = around, *ferre* = carry

Exploring word origins and histories builds both mathematical and literary understandings (Rubenstein and Thompson 2002; Rubenstein and Schwartz 2000; Thompson and Rubenstein 2000). It also builds an appreciation for the contributions of different cultures and highlights the human side of the history of mathematics.

Investigating the Symmetry of Regular Polygons

Other children commented on the symmetry of objects they saw in *So Many Circles, So Many Squares*. A third grader remarked about the centers of those same ventilation tubes: "Those lines across the circle make a dot, and that's the center, the middle." Another third grader commented on a square he saw on a vegetable basket: "If you put a line through that square, you'll have two triangles." These observations are significant because they underscore key ideas about symmetry and congruence: e.g., regular polygons have lines of symmetry; all lines of symmetry of regular polygons pass through the center; and lines of symmetry create congruent pieces.

Children in a fifth-grade class addressed the concept of rotational symmetry when they imagined the motion of a car wheel pictured on one page: "There's a diamond [actually a square tilted 45 degrees] inside that hubcap. If the car moves, and the side of that diamond moves to the top, then you could see it as a square." The context of a wheel moving enabled this child to rotate the shape successfully in her mind (see Figure 2.15). Analyzing the rotational symmetry of squares (and other regular polygons) highlights the different ways in which shapes can be transformed in space, such as through rotating, sliding, and flipping. It can also lead to an investigation of the interior angles of these polygons.

All of these observations related to symmetry can be the starting points for geometric explorations. Children's comments about the center of shapes can lead to a paper-folding investigation of regular polygons. See Appendix D for details of this activity. The fifth graders' interest in the rotation of a shape on a car wheel (rota-

Figure 2.15
Rotational Symmetry in the
Wheel of a Car

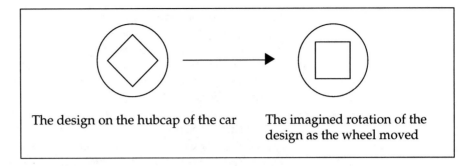

The design on the hubcap of the car

The imagined rotation of the
design as the wheel moved

tional symmetry) can also be extended. Children can cut out regular
polygons and explore ways to rotate and fit them into a cutout
frame. See Appendix E for detailed instructions for this investigation. Both of these activities build on what the children noticed and
push them to look more closely at the mathematical reasons behind
their observations.

Exploring the Area of
Irregular Shapes

In other classrooms, the photograph of a waffle stirred interesting
conversations. In a fifth-grade class (composed of many immigrant
children), none of the students had ever seen a waffle before. They
thought it was a cookie, were curious about its shape, and wanted to
count the squares inside it. A third-grade class also wanted to count
the squares and debated how to count the partial squares:

> *Child 1:* "There are 18 squares inside that waffle [counting whole
> squares]."
>
> *Child 2:* "I think there are more [counting the pieces of squares as
> other wholes]."
>
> *Child 3:* "But they are only little parts of squares."
>
> *Child 4:* "What if we counted like 18, plus pieces. That's like half a
> square, and another half, so that would be one more."

The students counted pieces and agreed that there were about 25 or
26 squares in the circle. This interest in counting squares on a waffle
is actually an interest in calculating area! Children gain a sense of
what area means when they have to find the areas of irregular
shapes, such as round waffles. Some beneficial extension experiences
include having children trace around their hand or foot on a piece of
centimeter paper and then determine its area. How will they count
the partial squares? Some children ignore them, others count any
partial square as 1/2, and others try to match smaller bits with larger
bits. Some even try to find a whole rectangle or square inside the
irregular space, calcuate its area, and then count the remaining
outside squares. It is important to discuss these different strategies
and analyze which ones are most accurate and most efficient. These

kinds of experiences help children understand what area is and how measurements are only approximations. Upper elementary students might investigate further the relationship between the area of circles and the area of squares that circumscribe those circles (*So Many Circles, So Many Squares* shows circular pipes encased in a square frame). Some of these activities are described in Appendix F.

In summary, these are a few activities that teachers might use to extend some of the mathematical ideas that children highlighted in *So Many Circles, So Many Squares.* A key strategy for using this book with *all* children is to keep the discussion open-ended so that students have the freedom to describe a range of mathematical ideas.

The Delight of Poetry across the Grades

Another way to explore mathematical and literary ideas across a wide age range is through poetry. It opens magical doors in any context, and the mathematics classroom is no exception. Poetry invites a playfulness with mathematical ideas. Children can laugh along with Eve Merriam as she pokes fun at the standard algorithm for division in "Gazinta" (1964). Poetry helps children appreciate how mathematics permeates everyday existence through poems such as Lee Bennett Hopkins's "School Bus" (1996) and Mary O'Neil's *Take a Number* (1968). Mathematical descriptions can evoke a sense of wonder and awe at the world as well. Readers marvel, for example, at the beauty of shape and form in nature that Barbara Esbensen illuminates in her collection *Echoes for the Eye* (1996). Math-related poetry can offer a fresh perspective on a unit of study, such as Alan Benjamin's "Let's Count the Raindrops" (2001) in a study of weather.

We have composed a list of individual poems that work well in the classroom, as well as a list of some anthologies (containing numerous math-related poems), specialized collections, and single poems in picture book format. These lists can be found at the end of the chapter. We invite you to enjoy these poems with your children during math class and throughout the day.

Viewing These Experiences through Language Arts and Mathematics Standards

Experiences rooted in the same book but explored by children from a wide range of ages demonstrate a fundamental belief that underpins both NCTM and NCTE/IRA Standards: Conceptual understanding begins early. Through children's experiences of many kinds and in many contexts, concepts become increasingly sophisticated, complex, and abstract. This evidence of the ongoing process of conceptual development, in both the English language arts and mathematics, is the strongest tie between the experiences described in this chapter and the Standards.

Children's investigations of *I Can Count the Petals of a Flower*

(Wahl and Wahl 1976) demonstrate several Standards from both mathematics (NCTM 2000) and English language arts (NCTE/IRA 1996). They recognized "connections among mathematical ideas" as well as applied "mathematics in contexts outside of mathematics" (NCTM Process Standards, Connections, p. 64). Students compared odd and even numbers with prime and composite numbers. Second-grade children compared multiplication (as repeated addition) with addition, while fourth graders explored the relationship between multiplication and division. Children also saw mathematical patterns and relationships in a scientific context; as a first grader aptly remarked, "This is a math and a science book!" Children conducted "research on issues and interests by generating ideas and questions" that arose from reading the book (NCTE/IRA Standard 7; see Table 1.1). First graders researched other flowers, fourth graders gathered statistics about animals, and sixth graders visited a greenhouse and consulted print and electronic resources to satisfy their curiosity (NCTE/IRA Standard 8). They represented their ideas through pictures, numerals, a 100-square chart, graphs, and written text for purposes of "communicating mathematical approaches, arguments, and understandings to one's self and to others" (NCTM Process Standards, Representation, p. 67). Finally, the book inspired interesting connections between mathematics and language arts. Fourth graders drew on their mathematical knowledge of primes to defend the authors' decision to conclude the book with 15 petals. Third graders made predictions about the second counting sequence, knowing that the authors must vary text to keep the reader's interest. Both of these classes were evaluating the text based on both their mathematical and their literary knowledge (NCTM Process Standards, Communication, p. 60; NCTE/IRA Standard 3). Many classes investigated the names of flowers, and a group of second graders came to appreciate that different languages have different alphabets (NCTE/IRA Standard 7).

Investigations stemming from *Two Greedy Bears* (Ginsburg 1998) demonstrate the Standards in other ways. Children of all ages applied the idea of one-half to a wide variety of contexts involving time, length, weight, area, and number. They explored the relationship between equivalence, symmetry, and congruence as they explained how the bears could ensure equal shares (NCTM Process Standards, Connections, p. 64). Second graders defended their solutions by naming the tools that could be used to verify equivalence, such as a scale or a ruler. Children from this second grade class as well as students from first and fourth grade used "different writing process elements," including humorous narrative, diagrams, pictures, and numbers, to communicate "for a variety of purposes" (NCTE/IRA Standard 5). When fifth-grade children talked about dividing homework "in half," they discovered that they needed to clarify which attribute mattered, time spent on homework or number of subjects (NCTM Process Standards, Communication, p. 60; NCTE/IRA Standard 4). Investigations of ratio demonstrated algebraic reasoning across the grades. Even kindergarten children showed their ability to "describe qualitative change" (NCTM Content Standards, Algebra, p. 90) when the dissatisfied bears wanted "*big* equal pieces" instead of "little crumbs." Fourth-grade children who investigated successive halving by folding paper were discovering "how a change in one variable [number of pieces] relates to a change in a second variable [size of each piece]" (NCTM Content Standards, Algebra, p. 158). From a language arts point of view, discussions about the story characters and theme contributed to "an understanding of the many dimensions of human experience" (NCTE/IRA Standard 2).

Experiences based on Tana Hoban's *So Many Circles, So Many Squares* (1998) offered many opportunities for children to develop understanding of and appreciation for language, as well as to analyze the properties of two- and three-dimensional geometric figures. Kindergartners and third graders noticed the relationship between squares and rhombi in the pictures of netting. These comments, as well as the other third graders' observations about a cube ("a puffed-up square") and a cone ("a pointy top, a circle at the bottom, and it curls all around"), show how "mathematical ideas interconnect and build on one another" (NCTM Process Standards, Connections, p. 64). In another language arts example, a fifth grader invented the term *squircle* to describe the unusual shapes made by a ventilation tube. Her terminology reflected her ability to draw on "prior experience" and "knowledge of word meaning" (NCTE/IRA Standard 3). All of these examples with language demonstrate a key tenet of the NCTM Communication Standard: "Allowing students to grapple with their ideas and develop their own informal means of expressing them can be an effective way to foster engagement and ownership" (p. 63).

Some important common threads run throughout all of these experiences. The books used in these classroom experiences shared some important characteristics. Each had themes, content, or formats that could appeal to a wide age range. The mathematical content was multilayered and subtly conveyed, so readers could investigate concepts and ideas with varying levels of sophistication. But even good books cannot guarantee rich conversations and investigations. The teachers you've met in the descriptions of these story investigations read and reread the books before showing them to their students. They considered the language arts and mathematical potentials. They knew of the many directions that follow-up investigations could take. Next, they shared the books with children, using open-ended questions such as, "What do you notice?" They listened, probed, challenged, and listened some more, opening the doors for meaningful learning.

References

Recommended Titles for a Wide Age Range

Following are lists of books featured in this chapter as well as others that can appeal to a wide range of ages.

Agee, Jon. *Jon Agee's Palindromania.* New York: Farrar, Straus and Giroux, 2002.

Aker, Suzanne. *What Comes in 2's, 3's, and 4's?* Illus. Bernie Karlin. New York: Simon & Schuster, 1990.

Anno, Mitsumasa. *Anno's Magic Seeds.* New York: Philomel, 1995.

Appelt, Kathi. *Bat Jamboree.* Illus. Melissa Scott. New York: Mulberry, 1998.

———. *Bats on Parade.* Illus. Melissa Sweet. New York: Morrow, 1999.

Birmingham, Duncan. *'M' Is for Mirror.* Norfolk, England: Tarquin, 1988.

Capucilli, Alyssa Satin. *Mrs. McTats and Her Houseful of Cats.* Illus. Joan Rankin. New York: Margaret K. McElderry Books, 2001.

Clement, Rod. *Counting on Frank.* Milwaukee, WI: Gareth Stevens, 1991.

Dee, Ruby, reteller. *Two Ways to Count to Ten: A Liberian Folktale.* Illus. Susan Meddaugh. New York: Henry Holt, 1988.

Demi. *One Grain of Rice.* New York: Scholastic, 1997.

Enzensberger, Hans Magnus. *The Number Devil: A Mathematical Adventure.* Illus. Rotraut Susanne Berner. Trans. Michael Henry Heim. New York: Henry Holt, 2000.

Facklam, Margery. *The Big Bug Book.* Illus. Paul Facklam. Boston: Little, Brown, 1994.

Franco, Betsy. *Grandpa's Quilt.* Illus. Linda A. Bild. New York: Children's Press, 1999.

Ginsburg, Mirra, adapter. *Two Greedy Bears.* Illus. Jose Aruego and Ariane Dewey. New York: Aladdin, 1998.

Guettier, Bénédicte. *The Father Who Had 10 Children.* New York: Dial, 1999.

Hamm, Diane Johnston. *How Many Feet in the Bed?* Illus. Kate Salley Palmer. New York: Simon & Schuster, 1991.

Harshman, Marc. *Only One.* Illus. Barbara Garrison. New York: Cobblehill Books/Dutton, 1993.

Hoban, Tana. *Look Book.* New York: Greenwillow Books, 1997.

———. *So Many Circles, So Many Squares.* New York: Greenwillow Books, 1998.

———. *26 Letters and 99 Cents.* New York: Scholastic, 1988.

Hong, Lily Toy, reteller. *Two of Everything: A Chinese Folktale.* Morton Grove, IL: Albert Whitman, 1992.

Hutchins, Pat. *The Doorbell Rang.* New York: Greenwillow Books, 1986.

Jenkins, Emily. *Five Creatures.* Illus. Tomek Bogacki. New York: Frances Foster Books, 2001.

Jenkins, Steve. *Looking Down.* Boston: Houghton Mifflin, 1997.

Johnson, Angela. *One of Three.* Illus. David Soman. New York: Orchard Books, 1995.

Lankford, Mary D. *Dominoes around the World.* Illus. Karen Dugan. New York: Morrow, 1998.

Lesser, Carolyn. *Spots: Counting Creatures from Sky to Sea.* Illus. Laura Regan. San Diego: Harcourt Brace, 1999.

MacDonald, Suse. *Look Whooo's Counting.* New York: Scholastic, 2000.

Marshall, Janet. *Look Once, Look Twice.* New York: Ticknor & Fields, 1995.

Mathews, Louise. *Gator Pie.* Illus. Jeni Bassett. Littleton, MA: Sundance, 1995.

McMillan, Bruce. *Jelly Beans for Sale.* New York: Scholastic, 1996.

Miller, Virginia. *Ten Red Apples: A Bartholomew Bear Counting Book.* Cambridge, MA: Candlewick Press, 2002.

Nagda, Ann Whitehead, and Cindy Bickel. *Tiger Math: Learning to Graph from a Baby Tiger.* New York: Henry Holt, 2000.

Pallotta, Jerry. *The Icky Bug Counting Book.* Illus. Ralph Mansiello. Watertown, MA: Charlesbridge, 1992.

Pinczes, Elinor J. *One Hundred Hungry Ants.* Illus. Bonnie MacKain. Boston: Houghton Mifflin, 1993.

———. *A Remainder of One.* Illus. Bonnie MacKain. Boston: Houghton Mifflin, 1995.

Pollock, Yevonne. *The Old Man's Mitten: A Traditional Tale.* Illus. Trish Hill. Glen Head, NY: Mondo, 1994.

Rice, David L. *Lifetimes.* Illus. Michael S. Maydak. Nevada City, CA: Dawn, 1997.

Ross, Catherine Sheldrick. *Circles: Shapes in Math, Science and Nature.* Illus. Bill Slavin. Toronto: Kids Can Press, 1992.

———. *Squares: Shapes in Math, Science and Nature.* Illus. Bill Slavin. Toronto: Kids Can Press, 1996.

———. *Triangles: Shapes in Math, Science and Nature.* Illus. Bill Slavin. Toronto: Kids Can Press, 1994.

Sayre, April Pulley, and Jeff Sayre. *One Is a Snail, Ten Is a Crab.* Illus. Randy Cecil. Cambridge, MA: Candlewick Press, 2003.

Schwartz, David M. *How Much Is a Million?* Illus. Steven Kellogg. New York: Lothrop, Lee & Shepard, 1985.

Schwartz, David M. *If You Hopped Like a Frog.* Illus. James Warhola. New York: Scholastic, 1999.

Scieszka, Jon. *Math Curse.* Illus. Lane Smith. New York: Viking, 1995.

Smith, David. *If the World Were a Village: A Book about the World's People.* Illus. Shelagh Armstrong. Toronto: Kids Can Press, 2002.

Sturges, Philemon. *Ten Flashing Fireflies.* Illus. Anna Vojtech. New York: North-South Books, 1995.

Tang, Greg. *Grapes of Math: Mind-Stretching Math Riddles.* Illus. Harry Briggs. New York: Scholastic, 2001.

Tompert, Ann. *Grandfather Tang's Story.* Illus. Robert Andrew Parker. New York: Crown, 1990.

Wahl, John, and Stacey Wahl. *I Can Count the Petals of a Flower.* Reston, VA: National Council of Teachers of Mathematics, 1976.

Walton, Rick. *How Many, How Many, How Many.* Illus. Cynthia Jabar. Cambridge, MA: Candlewick Press, 1993.

———. *So Many Bunnies: A Bedtime ABC and Counting Book.* Illus. Paige Miglio. New York: Lothrop, Lee & Shepard/Morrow, 1998.

Wells, Robert E. *What's Faster Than a Speeding Cheetah?* Morton Grove, IL: Albert Whitman, 1997.

Wyatt, Valerie. *The Math Book for Girls and Other Beings Who Count.* Illus. Pat Cupples. Toronto: Kids Can Press, 2000.

Zaslavsky, Claudia. *Math Games & Activities from around the World.* Chicago: Chicago Review Press, 1998.

———. *Number Sense and Nonsense: Building Math Creativity and Confidence through Number Play.* Chicago: Chicago Review Press, 2001.

Individual Poems

Benjamin, Alan. "Let's Count the Raindrops" (Viewing raindrops as large numbers) in *Let's Count the Raindrops.* Illus. Fumi Kosaka. New York: Viking, 2001.

Blair, Lee. "Using Subtraction" (Spoof on the term *take away*) in *Arithmetic in Verse and Rhyme,* sel. Allan D. Jacobs and Leland B. Jacobs. Champaign, IL: Garrard, 1971.

Ciardi, John. "Little Bits" (Dividing a pie into little bits and eating them all!) in *You Read to Me, I'll Read to You.* Philadelphia: Lippincott, 1962.

———. "How Much Is a Gross?" (Counting a gross of tennis shoes on kangaroos) in *Doodle Soup.* Boston: Houghton Mifflin, 1985.

Giovanni, Nikki. "Two Friends" (Counting pierced ears, pigtails, and more) in *Spin a Soft Black Song: Poems for Children.* New York: Hill and Wang, 1971.

Heide, Florence "Rocks" (Big rocks become millions of rocks over time) in *Small Talk: A Book of Short Poems,* sel. Lee Bennett Hopkins. San Diego: Harcourt Brace, 1995.

Hymes, Lucia, and James L. Hymes Jr. "Beans, Beans, Beans" (Classifying all kinds of beans) in *Hooray for Chocolate, and Other Easy-to-Read Jingles*. New York: W. R. Scott, 1960.

Merriam, Eve. "Gazinta" (A spoof on the division expression "goes into") in *It Doesn't Always Have to Rhyme*. New York: Atheneum, 1964.

———. "A Short Note" (Applying fractions to musical notation) in *It Doesn't Always Have to Rhyme*. New York: Atheneum, 1964.

Milne, A. A. "Halfway Down" (One-half is described as halfway down the stairs) in *When We Were Very Young*. New York: Dell, 1979.

Shields, Carol Diggory. "Eight-Oh-Three" (Hurrying to catch the school bus) in *Lunch Money and Other Poems about School*. New York: Dutton, 1995.

Anthologies, Specialized Collections, and Picture Book Poems

Brown, Margaret Wise. *Four Fur Feet*. Illus. Remy Charlip. New York: Dell, 1961/1990.

Esbensen, Barbara Juster. *Echoes for the Eye: Poems to Celebrate Patterns in Nature*. Illus. Helen K. Davie. New York: HarperCollins, 1996.

Franco, Betsy. *Mathematickles!* New York: Margaret K. McElderry Books, 2003.

Heide, Florence Parry, Judith Heide Gilliland, and Roxanne Heide Pierce. *It's about Time*. Illus. Cathryn Falwell. New York: Clarion Books, 1999.

Hopkins, Lee Bennett, selector. *Marvelous Math: A Book of Poems*. Illus. Karen Barbour. New York: Simon & Schuster, 1997.

———. *School Supplies: A Book of Poems*. Illus. Renée Flower. New York: Simon & Schuster, 1996.

———. *It's about Time*. Illus. Matt Novak. New York: Simon & Schuster, 1993.

Jacobs, Allan, and Leland Jacobs, selectors. *Arithmetic in Verse and Rhyme*. Illus. Kelly Oechsli. Champaign, IL: Garrard, 1971.

O'Neill, Mary. *Take a Number*. Illus. Al Nagy. Garden City, NY: Doubleday, 1968.

Prelutsky, Jack. *A Pizza the Size of the Sun*. Illus. James Stevenson. New York: Greenwillow Books, 1996.

Sandburg, Carl. *Arithmetic*. Illus. Ted Rand. San Diego: Harcourt Brace Jovanovich, 1993.

Silverstein, Shel. *A Giraffe and a Half*. New York: Harper & Row, 1964.

———. *The Missing Piece*. New York: Harper & Row, 1976.

———. *The Missing Piece Meets the Big O*. New York: Harper & Row, 1981.

———. *Where the Sidewalk Ends: The Poems & Drawings of Shel Silverstein*. New York: HarperCollins, 1974. ("Smart" is an all-time favorite poem.)

**Scholarly
Works Cited**

Golomb, Solomon W. *Polyominoes.* New York: Scribner, 1965.

Rubenstein, Rheta. "Word Origins: Building Communication Connections." *Mathematics Teaching in the Middle School* 5 (April 2000): 493–98.

Rubenstein, Rheta, and Randy K. Schwartz. "Word Histories: Melding Mathematics and Meaning." *Mathematics Teacher* 93, no. 8 (2000): 664–69.

Rubenstein, Rheta, and Denisse Thompson. "Understanding and Supporting Children's Mathematical Vocabulary Development." *Teaching Children Mathematics* 9, no. 2 (2002): 107–13.

Thompson, Denisse, and Rheta Rubenstein. "Learning Mathematics Vocabulary: Potential Pitfalls and Instructional Strategies." *Mathematics Teacher* 93, no. 7 (2000): 568–77.

Ventura, Jacqueline. "Integrating Literature, Mathematics, and Science." *Dialogues* (National Council of Teachers of Mathematics online) (January 2001, http://www.nctm.org/dialogues/2001-01/20010108_print.htm.

Walter, Marion I. *Boxes, Squares, and Other Things: A Teacher's Guide for a Unit in Informal Geometry.* Reston, VA: National Council of Teachers of Mathematics, 1970.

Whitin, David J., and Robin Cox. *A Mathematical Passage: Strategies for Promoting Inquiry in Grades 4–6.* Portsmouth, NH: Heinemann, 2003.

Whitin, Phyllis, and David J. Whitin. *Math Is Language Too: Talking and Writing in the Mathematics Classroom.* Urbana, IL: National Council of Teachers of English, and Reston, VA: National Council of Teachers of Mathematics, 2000.

3
Problem Posing with Children's Literature

This chapter looks at how teachers can use the strategy of problem posing in the context of children's literature. This strategy invites children to look closely at pieces of literature, describe features of those texts, and then extend or modify those attributes in interesting ways. Let's take a look at a few brief examples to show what problem posing looks like and to illustrate the potential benefits of this strategy.

In a second-grade class, Joanne Allinger asked her students what they noticed about a page from the concept book *26 Letters and 99 Cents* (Hoban 1988). On this particular page, different coins represent different amounts of money. One child commented, "I noticed that 26 has a quarter and a penny, but I can do it another way. I can do two dimes, one nickel, and one penny." Joanne responded, "How do you know those coins equal 26 cents?" The child reasoned, "Well, two dimes is 20 cents, and then five more cents is 25 cents, and then one more is 26." Joanne then invited others to join the investigation: "Are there other ways we can show 26 cents?" The children made a list of many other possibilities and then decided to do the same for other amounts of money illustrated in the book. Thus, Joanne helped initiate the investigation by challenging her students to look closely, pose their own questions, and extend the text.

In a kindergarten classroom, teacher Rebeka Eston was reading *Ten Black Dots* (Crews 1986). When she shared the page showing two open hands with three dots in each hand, one child observed, "Three plus 3 makes 6." Rebeka extended this observation by asking the class, "What else makes 6?" (Dacey and Eston 1999). The children then listed other two-addend combinations for 6. In a fourth-grade class, students were amazed that it took only 23 days to count to one million as described by David M. Schwartz in *How Much Is a Million?* (1985). They raised numerous questions: "What if we tried counting ourselves; would we get the same answer? What if we counted by 2s, 3s, or 4s; how long would it take us? What if we used a calculator to help us count?" (Schwartz and Whitin 1998). Here the children extended the text by devising their own investigations to pursue.

In all of these examples, children were engaging in the art of problem posing (Brown and Walter 1983/1990). This strategy consists of describing, extending, and modifying the attributes of a problem or story situation. Brown and Walter argue that these kinds of modifications open up "new vistas" in the way we think about common situations; a seemingly ordinary event can become quite extraordinary when looked at through a problem-posing lens. A photograph of coins, for instance, is transformed into a hunt for other possible coin combinations; an illustration of dots in a pair of hands invites an exploration of other two-addend pairs to equal six; and a fascinating question about counting to one million turns into further explorations of different ways to count.

Problem Posing Can Arise from Concept Books

Here are some possibilities:
 	
• *Let's Count* (Hoban 1999)
  What are other ways we can show the number 12?
 	
• *Numbers* (Hendra 1999)
  What other animals have special numbers?
 	
• *What Comes in 2's, 3's, and 4's?* (Aker 1990)
  What else in the world comes in sets of 2, 3, and 4?

Now let's examine this strategy more closely to see how other teachers have engaged their students in problem posing through a range of fiction and nonfiction titles. This chapter is organized in the following manner:

- Showing how this strategy can open up new possibilities with an old favorite, *The Doorbell Rang* (Hutchins 1986)

- Describing how teachers fostered a spirit of problem posing in five different ways

- Examining how the concept of doubling was explored in different ways across grades 2, 4, and 6

- Relating the benefits of this strategy to mathematics and English language arts Standards

Getting Started with Problem Posing: *The Doorbell Rang*

This chapter discusses several ways that teachers can engage children in extending a piece of literature through problem posing. But before discussing these classroom stories, let's do some problem posing ourselves. One of the best ways for teachers to envision some of the possibilities of a piece of literature is to list the mathematical features of the story and then record ways to modify them. Of course, teachers still want to listen to their students, ask open-ended questions, and be ready to explore in perhaps another direction. Having a chart of possibilities, however, provides a general sense of potential directions and helps teachers develop a mind-set for always extending mathematical tasks.

Let's take a look at a familiar math-related story to see how we can open it up in ways that expose some interesting mathematical territory. *The Doorbell Rang* (Hutchins 1986) tells the story of an increasing number of children who share 12 cookies. First 2 children divide up the cookies; then there are 3 children, then 4, 6, and 12. Before more children come, Grandma arrives with a large plate of cookies and all ends happily (even kindergartners realize that those cookies would have to be broken if Grandma hadn't arrived). Several attributes of this story might be interesting to explore. Let's examine a few possibilities.

1. Attribute: The numbers of cookies and children are equivalent at the end of the story (12).
   Modify: What if these numbers were not equivalent?
   Problem: How would 2 children share 5 cookies? How would 4 children share 13 cookies? How would 8 children share 6 cookies?

2. Attribute: The children share the cookies equally.
   Modify: What if they did not share the cookies equally?
   Problem: How many different ways can 2 children share 6 cookies? What if older children got twice as many cookies as younger children? How would 2 older children and 2 younger children share 12 cookies?

3. Attribute: The children kept arriving empty-handed.
   Modify: What if the children arrived with cookies to share?
   Problem: Suppose 2 children had 12 cookies. What if 2 more children arrived, each bringing 4 more cookies to share? How would all the children share those cookies?

4. Attribute: The cookies are all the same kind.
   Modify: What if there were chocolate chip cookies and oatmeal cookies?
   Problem: In what different ways could 2 children share 3 chocolate chip cookies and 3 oatmeal cookies?

5. Attribute: The children refrained from eating the cookies even as the doorbell rang.
   Modify: What if the children ate some of the cookies occasionally?
   Problem: What if each child ate 2 cookies every time the doorbell rang? What would happen if 2 children had 12 cookies and the doorbell rang? How many cookies would be left? What if 2 more children then entered the house and the doorbell rang again? How many cookies would be left now?

Listing and modifying attributes is one important way that teachers can think about the mathematical possibilities of stories.

The remainder of this chapter looks at specific ways teachers can use literature to develop a problem-posing stance in their class-

Figure 3.1
How to Support Problem-
Posing Investigations

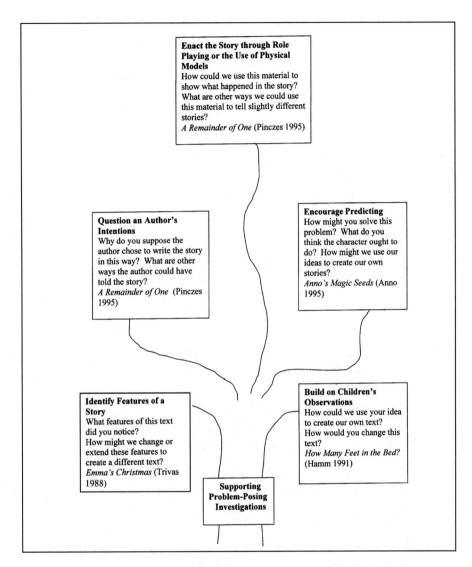

rooms. We relate classroom anecdotes in which teachers use the following strategies with their students:

1. They invite children to identify features of a story and propose alternative possibilities.

2. They listen carefully and build on children's spontaneous observations and questions.

3. They encourage children to make predictions about the story.

4. They ask children to question an author's intentions.

5. They challenge children to use models to enact the story (see Figure 3.1).

These strategies are not meant to be mutually exclusive. In fact, several of them are evident in each of the classroom anecdotes that follow. We list them separately here merely to highlight the unique features of each one. Throughout this chapter, we also note how responding to literature in this way can highlight not only mathematical benefits for children but also language arts ones as well.

Fostering a Spirit of Problem Posing
Identifying the Mathematical Features of a Story

One way that students can extend a math-related story is to list its attributes and then modify them in ways they find intriguing. We just practiced this strategy together with *The Doorbell Rang*. Let's see what it looks like when we encourage children to do this same kind of problem posing. Christie Forrest used this strategy with her fifth graders when she shared *Emma's Christmas* (Trivas 1988), which is an adaptation of "The Twelve Days of Christmas." In this version, a prince tries to woo the hand of a farmer's daughter, Emma, by sending a series of gifts each day: On the first day, he sends a partridge in a pear tree; on the second day, he sends two turtle doves and another partridge in a pear tree; on the third day, he sends three French hens, two more turtle doves, and still another partridge in a pear tree. And so the story continues until twelve days have passed. At the end of that time, Emma agrees to the marriage as long as they live on her farm! The prince agrees and all ends happily. Students who hear this story are often intrigued with the number of gifts Emma must have received. As Christie completed the story, Ashley posed that very question: "I wonder how many things she got in all. I know it was a lot!" Christie invited the children to figure out the total. When they shared their results, many reasoned that the answer was 78 (the sum of the first 12 numbers). But Ashley said, "I got 364. It might be too much." As she shared her work and explained her reasoning, it made good sense to her peers:

Try Problem Posing around an Interesting Statistic

For instance, the life expectancy for some animals includes:

Mouse	up to 6 years
Trout	up to 10 years
Rabbit	up to 13 years
Dog	up to 20 years
Tiger	up to 26 years
Cow	up to 30 years
Polar bear	up to 38 years
Bison	up to 40 years
Rhinoceros	up to 50 years
Hippopotamus	up to 54 years
Dolphin	up to 65 years
Human	up to 72 years
Indian elephant	up to 77 years
Giant tortoise	up to 100 years

- What if we compared mammals to reptiles?

- What if we compared life expectancy to number of offspring?

- What if we examined the life expectancy of humans in different countries?

Source: Russell Ash, *Incredible Comparisons* (New York: DK, 1996).

1	2	3	4	5	6	7	8	9	10	11	<u>12</u>
1	2	3	4	5	6	7	8	9	10	<u>11</u>	**12**
1	2	3	4	5	6	7	8	9	<u>10</u>	**22**	
1	2	3	4	5	6	7	8	<u>9</u>	**30**		
1	2	3	4	5	6	7	<u>8</u>	**36**			
1	2	3	4	5	6	<u>7</u>	**40**				
1	2	3	4	5	<u>6</u>	**42**					
1	2	3	4	<u>5</u>	**42**						
1	2	3	<u>4</u>	**40**							
1	2	<u>3</u>	**36**								
1	<u>2</u>	**30**									
<u>1</u>	**22**										
12											

"See, first I started with the last day and put all the gifts she got on this first line (pointing to her first horizontal line). Then I did day 11 with everything but the 12, and on and on to the first day. Then I added all the 1s, all the 2s, all the 3s, and kept going, then added all of those and got 364." Another student, Tiffany, then shared her results; she had used the same strategy but formatted the solution in a different way:

$$1 \times 12 = 12$$
$$2 \times 11 = 22$$
$$3 \times 10 = 30$$
$$4 \times 9 = 36$$
$$5 \times 8 = 40$$
$$6 \times 7 = 42$$
$$7 \times 6 = 42$$
$$8 \times 5 = 40$$
$$9 \times 4 = 36$$
$$10 \times 3 = 30$$
$$11 \times 2 = 22$$
$$12 \times 1 = 12$$

This different form of representation helped the children see the ascending and descending order of the factors. They also noted that the answers were "flipped," thereby highlighting the commutative property of multiplication, e.g., $1 \times 12 = 12 \times 1$, $2 \times 11 = 11 \times 2$, and so on. Tiffany had not noticed the symmetry of the products and commented later, "I didn't see that before I added all of them. I could have only added once and then doubled it!" (i.e., $12 + 22 + 30 + 36 + 40 + 42 = X$, and then doubled X to ascertain the final sum).

This initial problem solving, set in motion by the question of one child, stirred up even more interest in this gift-giving venture. Christie wanted the children to examine some other problem-posing possibilities so she asked them to list a few of the mathematical features, or attributes, of this story and how they might change them. Here is what their chart looked like:

Attribute of the Story	Changes
1. Gifts were given for 12 days.	1. What if gifts were given for 20, 13, or 10 days?
2. Gifts were repeated each day.	2. What if the gifts were not repeated? What if the gifts were doubled each day?

Sara decided not to repeat the same gifts each day and posed the problem of calculating the sum of $1 + 2 + 3 + \ldots + 12$. She was surprised to find the familiar answer of 78, which was the original, but incorrect, solution to the initial problem. She commented, "I guess we were kind of right that first time if we had just been counting the one gift a day. But in the story she kept on getting the same gifts every day. Like the turtle doves she got the second day, but then she got them every day after that too, not just the second day." By examining this particular problem variation, Sara gained a renewed appreciation for her peers' first solution strategy. Problem posing enables learners to make connections between a host of related problems so that they focus on relationships rather than isolated examples.

Tiffany shared her problem-posing variation next. She wanted to calculate the total number of gifts by doubling the number each day for 12 days (1, 2, 4, 8, 16, 32, 64, 128, 256, 512, 1,024, 2,048). As she explained her actual procedure to the class, however, it became apparent that she had not followed this strategy of doubling consistently. She began with 24 gifts the first day and doubled that number to obtain 48 gifts on the second day. At this point, she stopped doubling. Instead, she merely added the multiple of 24 gifts to each day that followed. Her sequence of numbers looked like this: 24, 48, 72, 96, 120, 144, 168, 192, 216, 240, 264, 288. As Tiffany shared these results with the class, she realized her error. But, in a wonderful problem-posing manner, she changed her question to match the sequence of numbers she had actually created: "Well, I could say that if she started with 24 gifts on day one, and then kept getting 24 gifts each day for 12 days, what would the total number be?" The class agreed that this indeed was the problem she was answering. Tiffany's example did highlight for the children the dramatic difference between an arithmetic and a geometric progression. It also demonstrated how mistakes can become sites for further learning.

Listening Carefully to Children's Observations and Questions

Listening to children's observations of math-related stories can often provide teachers the direction in which to go next. This point came to life for kindergarten teacher Cristina Azevedo when she read aloud *How Many Feet in the Bed?* (Hamm 1991). This is the story of a family who count the number of feet they have as they tumble in and out of bed on a Saturday morning. Dad begins the count with "two" and is joined successively by his daughter, son, infant, and wife. Cristina's class enjoyed predicting what the total number of feet was going to be as soon as the next person joined the group. At this point in the story, Cristina showed the children that she had read only half the story and asked them what they thought was going to happen next. Rabneet said, "I think their friends are going to come and we have to count more feet." Kashif responded, "I think they are going to count their toes now." The children then wanted to count their own toes and proceeded to count by fives around the circle. By encouraging the children to brainstorm what might happen next and then following up on the children's ideas, Cristina extended the story in a way that was meaningful to the class. As the story continues, a series of incidents, such as the ringing of the phone and the overflowing of the bathtub, force family members to leave the bed one by one (or two by two, if you are counting feet!).

As the story concluded, Alex asked, "What if we didn't have people on the bed but we had dogs?" Cristina had thought the story could lend itself to different ways of counting and was pleased that the children noted this same potential. She capitalized on this problem-posing extension by saying, "What a great question, Alex. That would make a wonderful story. Let's write our own story! So, are we going to count feet?" Elizabeth responded, "No, no, we have to count paws now." Cristina recorded the children's ideas and drew some paws as they dictated the story. Alex began: "Once upon a time there was a Papa dog that jumped on the bed to go to sleep." Jessica continued, "Then the baby puppy jumped on the bed and there were, hmmm, I don't know how many paws." Cristina finished drawing the next four paws, and Jessica correctly counted 8. Krystal then dictated the third page: "Then Clifford jumped on the bed. Ms. Azevedo, he has to be big and red!" Sukhoor continued: "Then Mama dog jumped on the bed and there were soooo many paws." The children counted 16. Kaitlyn concluded the story: "Then the girl puppy, Stephanie, went to sleep on the bed." They counted the total of 20. The numbers from the original story and the numbers from the children's story could now be compared: 2, 4, 6, 8, 10 and 4, 8, 12, 16, 20. The children noticed that counting by 4s "went higher" than counting by 2s. With

---

Listen for Children's Spontaneous Observations and Questions

These can often be the catalyst for an exploration. Some responses include:

- "I bet I can count to 10 faster than that." (*Two Ways to Count to Ten* [Dee 1988])

- "How come that book is called a square?" (*Sea Squares* [Hulme 1991])

- "How does that math trick work?" (*Number Sense and Nonsense* [Zaslavsky 2001])

Number Sense and Nonsense

Building Math

Creativity and

Confidence

Through

Number Play

Claudia Zaslavsky

Cristina's guidance, they also saw that counting by 4s landed on every other multiple of 2. Listing the multiples underneath each other helped to show this relationship:

2, 4, 6, 8, 10, 12, 14, 16, 18, 20

4,   8,   12,   16,   20

One child remarked that they could really count the sets of animals' legs by 2s. In her own way, she was saying that multiples of 4 are a subset of multiples of 2. This important relationship emerged because the children had created their own problem variation.

Kaitlyn next asked, "What if we used worms in the bed?" Cristina realized that the children were enjoying the opportunity to suggest other problem-posing possibilities. Therefore, she invited them to create their own stories and worked with different children during center time. Cristina's conversation with Kashif demonstrated how a child might problem pose with both the mathematical and literary aspects of a story. As he began to write, Kashif told Cristina, "I don't really want to write about dogs." She responded, "What else can you write about?" He said, "I can write about cats, or elephants, or birds, but they don't sleep in a bed." Cristina agreed, saying, "Your story doesn't have to have a bed in it. It can take place

Figure 3.2
Kashif's Mathematical and
Language Arts Extension of
How Many Feet in the Bed?

anywhere you want." Relieved, Kashif said, "I'm going to write about birds, and I'm going to put them in a tree where they live. And I'm going to count the feet." He titled his book "Birds" and tallied the total on each page by writing, "2 feet in the tree; 4 feet in the tree; 6 feet in the tree" (Figure 3.2). His story nicely reflects the strategy of problem posing. He continued to count by 2s but changed the context of the story to do so. Kashif was gaining both mathematical and literary insights. He created another predictable story by using the linguistic structure of the read-aloud, and he continued the mathematical pattern of counting by 2s. Problem posing with literature offers children both of these kinds of opportunities.

    Marie Vinel found this same kind of natural problem posing by children when she shared *Only One* (Harshman 1993) with seven-year-old Deidre. This story uses a predictable, poetic format to describe sets of things in the world. As Marie began to read the story aloud, she was amazed to hear Deidre modify the text of each page. The story opens, "There may be 50,000 bees but there is only one hive." Deidre responded, "There may be 10 jars of honey but there is only one hive." She continued to offer her own variation to the text as Marie read aloud other pages:

Text: There may be 500 seeds but there is only one pumpkin.

Deidre: There may be 1 pumpkin but you need 2 spoons to scoop out the seeds.

Text: There may be 500 patches but there is only 1 quilt.

Deidre: There may be 2 colors but there is only 1 quilt.

Text: There may be 12 eggs but there is only 1 dozen.

Deidre: There may be 12 doughnuts but there is only 1 dozen.

Text: There may be 5 babies but there is only 1 nest.

Deidre: There may be 5 fish but there is only 1 school; and there may be 12 piglets but there is only 1 litter. See, there may be 4 feet but there is only 1 chair, and there may be 4 feet but there is only 1 rabbit. The word *kids* has doubles too [double meaning]. Look: there may be 4 kids but there is only 1 daddy, and there may be 4 kids but there is only 1 goat.

Text: There may be one life, but there is only one me and there is only one you.

Deidre: No matter how long you live, there's only 1 life.

Deidre was clearly having fun innovating off the text. She naturally engaged in the art of problem posing as she extended the text by offering some suitable substitutions. The book described sets of things in the world, and Deidre offered her own ideas of sets while still maintaining the structure of the text. She even discussed the meaning of collective nouns (perhaps prompted by the word *dozen* in the text). Her responses offer opportunities to find other collective nouns, list more examples of sets of things, and build ratio tables (5 babies, 1 nest; 10 babies, 2 nests; etc.). Here again a child's natural inclination to extend a text provided some rich mathematical ground to cover. Engaging and well-written texts can yield these important benefits.

Another example of problem posing emerging from the children's observations came from a kindergarten classroom. Theresa Dowdican was reading aloud *The King's Commissioners* (Friedman 1994). In this story, a king fears that he has been appointing too many royal commissioners whenever he needs help. With the assistance of two loyal advisors, he proceeds to count all of his employees. At first he tries to count by 1s, but he loses track. Then the first royal advisor counts by 2s and finds the answer to be twenty-three 2s plus one more. The second royal

---

Some Predictable Stories That Invite Talk of Mathematical Possibilities:

- *How Many Snails?* (Giganti 1988)
  What if we counted this page in another way?

- *Spots: Counting Creatures from Sky to Sea* (Lesser 1999)
  What if we made a story about creatures with stripes?

- *Ten Flashing Fireflies* (Sturges 1995)
  What if the children caught 2 fireflies at a time (not just 1)?

advisor, counting by 5s, arrives at nine 5s plus two more. The king is angered by the apparent difference in the answers, but his daughter explains how the answers are really equivalent. The children were fascinated by the problem of this story, and one child asked, "I wonder if you could count another way and get none left over." Theresa gave them sets of snap cubes, and they worked on the problem, snapping together sets of other numbers to see if they could find a number that did not yield a remainder (which they couldn't since 47 is a prime number). But Theresa pursued the children's interest in leftovers again the next day. She gave each child 10 Unifix cubes and asked them if they could make three towers of equal height using all the cubes. After several attempts, they said they just kept getting leftovers, like the problem they had encountered the previous day. Theresa then challenged them with the following problem: "See if you can make equal towers with these 10 cubes so that you don't have any leftovers." This problem built on their earlier interest in partitioning the 47 cubes into equal groups. The children tried different combinations until they found 2 sets of 5 and 5 sets of 2. "Hey, it's just like this," one child observed, and moved his hands and arms across each other to show that the two solutions were the reverse of each other. His motions nicely conveyed the commutative property of multiplication. Thus, the children used manipulatives, oral language, and gesturing to convey this important relationship. Finally, the teacher played a key role in fostering this problem-posing stance. Theresa listened to her students' natural inquisitiveness about the story problem, invited them to try to solve it themselves, and then extended the problem by using some smaller numbers.

Encouraging Children to Make Predictions

By encouraging children to make predictions about stories and then compare those predictions to the author's actual decisions, teachers can often open up problem-posing opportunities. Amanda Morrison used this strategy with her sixth-grade students as she shared *Anno's Magic Seeds* (Anno 1995). In this story, a man named Jack receives two magic seeds from a wizard. By eating one of these magic seeds, Jack would not grow hungry for a whole year. By planting a seed, he would grow a tree that would yield two more seeds. This story describes the decisions Jack makes about this unusual gift. Before Amanda began reading the story, she explained the potential benefits of these seeds and asked the children what decisions they would make with such a gift. She was curious to see if they would be able to consider a range of alternatives. She later related her thoughts on this strategy: "I wondered if they would realize that if they didn't eat any of the seeds for a year that they would be able to grow more seeds. Did they realize that there were different possibilities of what they could do?" After a brief discussion, the children agreed that it would be best to eat one seed and plant the other so that this cycle could continue forever. Amanda decided not to raise any other possibilities at this time and instead began reading the story. The children listened intently and nodded their heads in a self-congratulatory way as Jack began to make the decision they had predicted. As the story progressed, however, and he decides not to eat any seeds for a year, there was a group chorus of "Oooh yeah!" The children suddenly realized that there were other possibilities. One student shouted out, "Now he's going to have four seeds! I didn't think about it that way." Other children nodded in agreement. By offering their own predictions first, the children were particularly interested in the character's (and author's) decision.

Before continuing with the story, Amanda said, "Turn and discuss with your partner what Jack can do next year with four seeds." After some small group brainstorming, the children generated many possibilities. These four ideas seemed the most plausible to them:

1. Plant all 4 seeds. Next year he would have 8.
2. Eat one seed and plant 3. Next year he would have 6.
3. Eat 1 seed, plant 1 seed, and save 2 seeds. Next year he would have 4.
4. Eat 1 seed, plant 2 seeds, and save 1 seed. Next year he would have 5.

Together the children decided that the second alternative was the best decision because Jack would have the maximum number of seeds without being hungry. Amanda then continued to read, and the children learned that, indeed, Jack kept planting more and more seeds. Although an unexpected storm destroyed almost all of his trees, he still found a few seeds to begin his planting once again. As she closed the book, Amanda invited the children's comments about the story. Jarrett said he hadn't realized how many different ways there were to think about the seeds. Sammy said he liked the story because he wanted to figure out what Jack was going to do next. This encouragement to predict enabled the children to envision other possible decisions the author could have made.

A natural follow-up to this discussion was to invite the children to create their own version of this multiplying story. Alex wrote a story entitled "The Mysterious Multiplying Money" that described a little boy who received $5.00 for his birthday. Every dollar the boy saved would double each day. But the boy had to spend *at least* $2.00 each day so that "he could have some fun with the money and not have to save it all." In the story (Figure 3.3), Joseph starts out with $5.00 on Monday and continues to accumulate and spend his money in the following manner:

Day	Doubling	Money Spent/Remainder
Monday	$5.00	
Tuesday	$10.00 ($5 × 2)	$10.00 – $2.00 = $8.00
Wednesday	$16.00 ($8 × 2)	$16.00 – $8.00 = $8.00
Thursday	$16.00 ($8 × 2)	$16.00 – $4.00 = $12.00
Friday	$24.00 ($12 × 2)	$24.00 – $2.00 = $22.00
Saturday	$44.00 ($22 × 2)	$44.00 – $2.00 = $42.00
Sunday	$84.00 ($42 × 2)	

On Thursday Joseph decides that he wants to buy a bike for $75.00, and so he begins to save with that goal in mind. By Sunday he has accumulated more than enough money to buy his bike. The story reflects how Alex took some of the attributes of Anno's story (doubling, saving and spending/eating) and transformed them into his own version by changing the context and the rules for how much of his money to keep and how much to spend. The teacher supported this problem-posing stance by her encouragement of predicting and her recording of possibilities. In this way, other options emerged, and children could imagine other mathematical results.

Inviting Children to Question an Author's Intentions

When children are invited to question an author's intentions in writing a given story, their analysis can often lead to problem-posing opportunities. This certainly happened in Victoria Connell's fourth-grade class when she read *A Remainder of One* (Pinczes 1995). In this story, 25 ants try to march in neat and tidy arrays before their queen. Poor soldier ant Joe, however, keeps being an unfortunate remainder. The ants try 2 rows of 12, 3 rows of 8, and 4 rows of 6, and each formation renders Joe a remainder every time. Finally, the story ends happily when the ants discover that 5 rows of 5 is the perfect solution. We have found that children enjoy this story for several reasons. They relate to Joe's plight of being alone and rejoice when he finds a way to join his friends in the "neat" and "tidy" formation of 5 × 5. Children also enjoy the predictable structure of the story. The repeating strains of Joe's predicament are captured with such phrases as, "All 25 soldiers passed by the bug crowd / nervously hoping they'd make their queen proud. / The troop had divided by three for the show; / Each line seemed perfect. / Then someone spied Joe" (unpaged). Thus, the children's emotional attachment to Joe's plight often leads them to look closely at the mathematical aspects of his problem.

Figure 3.3
Alex's Extension of Anno's Magic Seeds

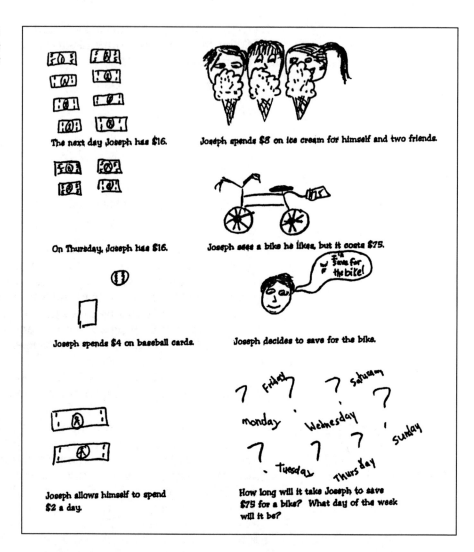

The next day Joseph has $16.

Joseph spends $8 on ice cream for himself and two friends.

On Thursday, Joseph has $16.

Joseph sees a bike he likes, but it costs $75.

Joseph spends $4 on baseball cards.

Joseph decides to save for the bike.

Joseph allows himself to spend $2 a day.

How long will it take Joseph to save $75 for a bike? What day of the week will it be?

The children noted that the author "kept putting the bugs in lines" because it was "easier to see if there was a remainder that way." At this point, Victoria discussed that mathematicians often use arrays (rectangular arrangements of rows and columns) to show number relationships. The children immediately made connections to this idea with their own personal examples of arrays: base ten blocks, ceiling tiles, clusters of desks, and windowpanes. It was the children's observation of the author's decision to use arrays that prompted them to make these personal connections.

Victoria continued to challenge the children to explore some of the problem-posing possibilities of the story. She invited them to analyze the author's intentions when she asked, "Why do you suppose the author chose to use the number 25 in *A Remainder of One*?" Alejandra responded, "I think she wanted to have a remainder." Victoria kept pushing the question, "Why 25? Why not another number?" Mary reasoned, "It's odd so it has a better chance of having a remainder." Victoria countered, "So do you think all odd numbers would be good numbers?" Children tried out a few numbers to see and then Cameron shared his thoughts: "No, some odd numbers aren't as good because they can't be divided evenly at all. Like 13. I tried 13 and it didn't work." (At this point, Victoria briefly discussed the work the children had done earlier in the year with prime and composite numbers.) Katherine then added, "If the author had picked an even number, the story would have been over real quick because it would divide evenly. It wouldn't even have a problem. So I think the number [the author uses] has to be odd." Michael refined that suggestion: "I think 25 is a good number because it is both odd and composite." Margi suggested that they try 27 because it too is odd and composite, but Alejandra immediately responded, "Yeah, but the story would be over after they divided by 3. I tried 45 and that was the same problem." Fernando offered another idea: "I think the number needs to be a square [number]." Tika suggested that 49 might be a good choice because it was odd, composite, and square. When the children tested this number, they found:

> 49/2 = 24 R1
> 49/3 = 16 R1
> 49/4 = 12 R1

They were pleased that they had discovered three consecutive remainders of one. But when they tried 49/5, they encountered a problem that Ben described: "Well, they wouldn't be able to call it *A Remainder of One*, because when you get to dividing it by 5 there is a remainder of 4!" The rest of the class laughed at the unexpected result. On further analysis, they realized that the number needed to end in 0 or 5 since it needed to be a multiple of 5 to divide evenly. Further testing yielded the number 85.

> 85/2 = 42 R1
> 85/3 = 28 R1
> 85/4 = 21 R1
> 85/5 = 17

Invite Children to Question an Author's Decisions about the Mathematics in the Text

Some books for questioning an author's intentions include:

- *Bats on Parade* (Appelt 1999)
  Why did the author choose these numbers for marching bands?
- *The Grapes of Math* (Tang 2001)
  Why did the author pick these numbers for counting?
- *The Great Divide* (Dodds 1999)
  Why did the author start the story with 80 racers?

In summary, the children's questioning of the author's intentions highlighted the idea that authors have options. Examining and testing some of these options underscores for children what problem posing is all about. Victoria played a key role in making this investigation happen by pushing the children to confront the uniqueness of 25. Her questioning propelled the exploration forward, helping the students revisit their previous work with odds, evens, factors, primes, and composites.

Creating a Model of Some Mathematical Ideas in a Story

Creating models for mathematical ideas in a story can also lead to problem-posing extensions. Joyce Porter used this strategy with some fourth-grade students as she read aloud this same story, *A Remainder of One* (Pinczes 1995). As Joyce read aloud the story a second time, she invited the children to use beans as counters and to act out the story. It is interesting to see how an investigation very different from the one in Victoria Connell's class emerged.

When Joyce read the part about dividing into three rows, most children used the beans to show 3 rows of 8. Brittany, however, made a very different arrangement: she created two arrays and placed them next to each other, 2 × 8 and 3 × 3. She said, "This is the way I would march the ants." Using the beans helped Brittany experiment with other possibilities and set the direction for a different kind of problem. Other students asked, "Can we do it that way?" Joyce realized that Brittany's alternative solution opened up a new problem to explore, and so she responded, "That's an interesting solution. What if we thought about using *two* arrays so that all 25 ants were included? What answers might we find?" The children decided they wanted to make arrays that had at least two rows; they didn't like the appearance of just single lines. They found these solutions for 25: 3 × 3 and 4 × 4; 7 × 3 and 2 × 2; and 8 × 2 and 3 × 3.

> **Some Books That Can Lead to Acting Out Mathematical Scenarios:**
> - *Grandpa's Quilt* (Franco 1999)
>   Let's show different quilts using 36 squares.
> - *How Hungry Are You?* (Napoli and Tchen 2001)
>   Let's try sharing this food in different ways.
> - *The Number Devil* (Enzensberger 2000)
>   Let's try acting out the different seating arrangements for 3 children.
> - *Two of Everything* (Hong 1992)
>   Let's pretend we have a magic doubling pot.

```
x x x   x x x x   x x x x x x x   x x   x x x x x x x x   x x x
x x x   x x x x   x x x x x x x   x x   x x x x x x x x   x x x
x x x   x x x x   x x x x x x x          x x x
        x x x x

3 × 3    4 × 4       7 × 3       2 × 2      8 × 2         3 × 3
```

The students were intrigued that they had made so many square numbers. Although the children did not pursue this problem any further, they had opened up other questions to explore: What if we tried using three different arrays? What if we tried using other square numbers, such as 36, 49, and 64? What numbers have the most square arrays inside them? Problem posing raises more questions than it answers. This realization is an important one for children as they assume more ownership for formulating their own mathematical problems.

Problem Posing with One Concept across Different Grades

In concluding this chapter, we would like to highlight one additional benefit of problem posing. This strategy enables students with a range of abilities and experiences to explore the same mathematical concept. By using the familiar context of stories, and by inviting children to modify the mathematics of these stories, teachers can more easily create new mathematical opportunities for all learners. To demonstrate this point, let's look at a set of books that portray the mathematical concept of doubling (or geometric progression). The following chart summarizes how teachers in grades 2, 4, and 6 extended this concept in interesting ways with their students:

Attribute of the Stories	Extension	Benefit
1. The numbers doubled.	1. What if we tripled the numbers? (grade 4)	1. Comparison of progressions
2. The numbers that were doubled were consecutive.	2. What if we doubled numbers that were not consecutive and added them? (grade 2)	2. Calculating equivalent sums for 100
3. The sum for each day was double the previous day's total.	3. What if we added the sum of each day to obtain a running total? (grade 6)	3. Noting patterns across data

Cindy Parker used *The King's Chessboard* (Birch 1988) with her sixth-grade class. This book is a rendering of the well-known Indian folktale of a king who wishes to reward his grand counselor for all his wisdom over the years. The counselor does not wish any reward, but the king insists. Seeing a chessboard hanging on the wall, the counselor has an idea. He requests some rice for each square of the chessboard, but the rice must be allocated in a specific way: 1 grain of rice for the first square, then doubled to 2 grains of rice for the second square, then doubled again to 4 grains of rice for the third square, and so on for the 64 squares on the board. The king agrees to the bargain but with little thought for the mathematical consequences. Although the number of grains of rice starts out small, as it continues to double the king finally realizes that he does not own enough rice in the kingdom to grant the request. The king learns a lesson in humility as readers are introduced to the power of geometric progression.

After Cindy shared this book with her students, she found that they wanted to double the numbers themselves and see what they looked like more closely. When the numbers were recorded on the board, Natasha remarked, "Hey, that doesn't tell how many grains of rice altogether. It just tells the number for that day. We got to add up all the days before." Her observation provided a problem-posing extension for the class to pursue. They made a chart that contained some of these numbers:

Day	Grains	Total
1	1	1
2	2	3
3	4	7
4	8	15

5	16	31
6	32	63
7	64	127

The children noticed that the numbers for the total grains of rice were always odd and the numbers for the doubled grains of rice were even (except 1). They discussed how doubling a number (such as 8 × 2, or 16) and then adding an odd number (16 + 15) yields only an odd sum (31). They noticed that every other number of grains was a square number (4, 16, 64). This interest in squares led them to look at other nonsquare numbers. They found that some of these numbers (such as 8, 32, and 128) were a constant difference away from a square: 8 – 7 = 1; 32 – 7 = 25; 128 – 7 = 121. (The constant difference of 7 changes as the numbers get larger. For instance, 512 – 28 = 484 [22 × 22] and 2,048 – 23 = 2,025 [45 × 45].) Other children noticed that the difference between the number of grains of rice and the previous day's total was always 1: 2 – 1 = 1; 4 – 3 = 1; 8 – 7 = 1; and so on. They were intrigued with this pattern and asked, "What if we started with 4 grains of rice instead of 1—what would happen?" They created the following chart:

Date	Grains	Total
1	4	4
2	8	12
3	16	28
4	32	60

This time they found that the constant difference was 4: 8 – 4 = 4; 16 – 12 = 4; and 32 – 28 = 4. They realized that the beginning total gets added to the second day's total, always giving it a constant difference. Looking closely at the numbers from this story gave the students some interesting problem-posing extensions to pursue.

In a fourth-grade class, Phebbie Williams shared *A Grain of Rice* (Pittman 1986), which is another version of this doubling tale. As the children discussed the story, they became interested in things that doubled. They discussed expressions in which variations of the word *double* appeared, such as:

> Double bed
>
> Double check
>
> Double-decker (sandwich or bus)
>
> Double-digit
>
> Double dribble

What Multiplies by Dividing?

(bacteria, microbes, germs)

E. coli bacteria can double every 20 minutes (in a warm, moist environment). How long would it take 1 E. coli cell to produce 1,000 bacteria? Estimate the number of bacteria at the end of 10 hours. How close was your estimate?

Phebbie asked them, "What things in the world do we double?" Some of their ideas included:

Double a recipe

Double a fine

Bacteria doubles

Here again the language arts benefits merge with the mathematical ones as children explore the language of mathematics in meaningful contexts.

The children had learned in health class that some bacteria double every hour. Students now connected this piece of health information to the new context of an Indian folktale. Chris wanted to know how long it would take bacteria to reach one million bacteria if it doubled every hour. The children calculated that it would take 21 hours. This investigation sparked their interest, and Andrea asked, "How long would it take if it tripled?" They used calculators this time and found that it would take just 13 triples to cross the one million mark. They compared that rate to the doubling rate:

1	1
3	2
9	4
27	8
81	16
243	32
729	64
2,187	128
6,561	256
19,683	512
59,049	1,024
177,147	2,048
531,441	4,096
1,594,323	8,192

The children noticed that by the third term the 9 was more than twice the 4, and by the fourth term the 27 was more than three times greater than the 8. They saw how this multiplicative size difference kept getting larger as the terms of the progressions increased. (It would have been interesting to show an arithmetic progression as

Spreading Random Acts of Kindness around the World

Do something nice for two people you know. Now ask them to "pass on the favor" by doing something nice for 2 other people, asking those 4 people to do nice things for 2 other people. Those 8 people (since 4 × 2 = 8) then should be encouraged to help 16 more people (just 2 each, since 8 × 2 = 16). How many times would this doubling have to occur until you reached all 6 billion people in the world? (Not as many times as you might think.)

another example for comparison, e.g., 2, 4, 6, 8, 10, 12 . . .) The teacher played a key role in this investigation by inviting the children to brainstorm other contexts for doubling. Eventually, it was the children's fascination with bacteria doubling that led them to this extended exploration and comparison.

One last example involved a second-grade teacher, Mirella Rizzo, who read *Two of Everything* (Hong 1992) to her students. This is a folktale in which a poor farmer finds a magic pot that doubles everything he puts inside it. It causes him much happiness (he doubles his gold coins) but also much trouble (he himself falls into the pot, and later so does his wife!). The story ends happily as the two couples live next door to each other as identical neighbors. Mirella extended the mathematics of the story by challenging the children to find different ways of doubling numbers to make the sum of $1.00. This extension retained the attribute of doubling from the story but changed the context to money and put a restriction on the total amount. The problem was still open-ended enough to allow the children to respond in a variety of ways. Their solutions included:

- Double 50 to get 100.
- Double 25 to get 50, and then double 50 to get 100.
- Double 5 to get 10; then double 10 to get 20; then add 10 and 20 to get 30; double 30 to get 60. Then double 20 to get 40, and add 40 + 60 = 100.
- Double 25 to get 50; then double 20 to get 40; then double 5 to get 10. Now add 50 + 40 + 10 = 100.
- Double 5 to get 10. Do this 10 times, and then add the ten 10s to get 100.
- Double 5 to get 10; double 10 to get 20; double 20 to get 40. Now take away 15 cents, and then you have 25. Then double 25 to get 50, and double 50 to get 100.

Although these second graders did not double a continuous set of numbers in the true sense of a geometric progression, they did use the doubling property to increase amounts. In a follow-up discussion, the teacher highlighted the difference between the children's use of doubling only once and the continuous doubling of a true geometric progression.

All three of these classroom stories show how the same mathematical idea can be pursued in different ways. From a problem-posing perspective, these teachers and students modified some of the story attributes to create new challenges for themselves.

Try Some Doubling Experiments

1. If you started with $1.00 and doubled it every hour, how long would it take you to reach $1,000,000?

2. If you started with a one-foot length of string, how many times would you have to double its length to go around the equator (about 25,000 miles)?

3. If you started with a one-pound weight, how many doublings would it take to equal the weight of an elephant (an African elephant weighs about 6 tons, or 12,000 pounds)?

Viewing These Experiences through Mathematics and Language Arts Standards

Problem-posing opportunities can emerge quite naturally from children's literature. In some instances, the children suggest next steps, such as counting the feet of dogs or worms rather than human beings, as in *How Many Feet in the Bed?* In other cases, teachers can elicit some possibilities by asking children to make predictions, such as how a farmer might use his magic seeds; or list interesting features of a story, such as the gift-giving parameters of *Emma's Christmas*; or question an author's intentions, such as why Elinor Pinczes picked the number 25 to tell her story *A Remainder of One*. In other cases, teachers and students might extend the story together, such as teachers giving students materials to enact the story but watching for ways the children use these manipulatives in new ways.

The mathematical goals advocated by NCTM are also brought to life in these classrooms as all children are challenged to communicate, reason, question, debate, and represent their mathematical understandings. NCTM's *Principles and Standards for School Mathematics* (2000) describes mathematical thinking with active verbs such as *explore, investigate, conjecture, predict, explain, discover, construct, describe*, and so on. All of these verbs emphasize the importance of children making sense of mathematics for themselves. These verbs require children to be initiators, not receivers, of mathematical knowledge. Initiators pose problems, raise questions, offer hypotheses, and share their reasoning with peers.

These stories also reflect the kind of mathematical rigor advocated by NCTM's *Principles and Standards for School Mathematics* (2000): "All students should have the opportunity and the support necessary to learn significant mathematics with depth and understanding. There is no conflict between equity and excellence" (p. 5). NCTM's Equity Principle requires that all students have access to a "challenging mathematical curriculum." Problem posing allows learners the opportunity to stretch beyond a given problem and investigate a set of related problems. As an example, children in grades 2, 4, and 6 could all be exposed to the doubling principle through the context of a story. Literature is one way that mathematical ideas can be made more accessible to all learners.

Principles and Standards also emphasizes that learning mathematical content is always accompanied by learning mathematical attitudes and dispositions. Any given problem-solving situation has the potential to encourage positive or negative mathematical attitudes. Harmful attitudes, for instance, are sometimes fostered when children learn that they need to solve all math problems quickly, without the help of peers, and in only one prescribed way. The attitudes children acquire are just as important as the content they are learning. John Dewey (1938) described these attitudes as "collateral learning" because children literally learn them "side by side" (*latus* is the Latin word for "side") the content they are studying. The learners described in this chapter certainly demonstrate a range of important mathematical attitudes, such as risk-taking, perseverance, and skepticism.

Problem posing demonstrates the spiraling nature of inquiry learning, as learners see that observations beget further questions and that "every particular has a world within it" (Brown and Walter 1983/1990, p. 23). The words *what if* allow us to go beyond the present problem and entertain a host of related problems. They also foster a "spirit of adventure, intellectual excitement, and class unity" (p. 126) by legitimizing asking questions and freeing learners from the one-answer syndrome (p. 5). As stated earlier, these benefits are certainly consistent with the kind of supportive learning environment proposed in NCTM's *Principles and Standards.* In this environment, students are expected to question assumptions, challenge ideas, and extend mathematical observations. Problem posing can encourage this kind of investigative activity.

Other NCTM Standards are evident throughout this chapter as well. The Representation Standard is demonstrated as children generated different charts to show the number of gifts in *Emma's Christmas.* Children in a kindergarten class used manipulatives, oral language, and gesturing to represent commutativity in multiplication. NCTM's Connections Principle is illustrated by some fourth-grade children who connected prime and composite numbers to odd, even, and square numbers. Other fourth graders connected the doubling sequence of a story to the doubling of bacteria, which they had been learning about in science/health class. NCTM's Reasoning and Proof Standard and Communication Standard are evident as children determined another number like 25 that would have three remainder 1s in a row (*A Remainder of One*). They reasoned logically that this other number had to be odd, composite, and end in 0 or 5. A child's incorrect solution for totaling gifts (*Emma's Christmas*) provided her an opportunity to explain the difference between an arithmetic and a geometric progression. Thus, using literature as a context and problem posing as a strategy, teachers brought to life many of these NCTM Standards.

In a similar fashion, teachers provided students with many language arts benefits. Children gain important insights about an author's craft by analyzing an author's choices, examining the story structure, and discussing how problem-centered stories are constructed to make an entertaining tale. After children investigated other possible numbers for telling *A Remainder of One,* for instance, they better appreciated the intentional choices an author makes to extend the suspense of a story and postpone the resolution of the central problem. Another strategy that children used "to compre-

April Pulley Sayre and Jeff Sayre ✿ illustrated by Randy Cecil

hend, interpret, evaluate, and appreciate texts" (NCTE/IRA 1996, p. 3) was to predict what might happen next in a story. Kindergartners did this kind of predicting with *How Many Feet in the Bed?* and were able to understand the story's structure and sequence of events. Sixth graders also predicted with *Anno's Magic Seeds,* enabling them to better analyze and appreciate the range of possibilities the author could have entertained.

This kind of analysis of story structure influenced the writing the children did. A kindergartner used the pattern of counting by 2s *(How Many Feet in the Bed?)* to create his own story about birds. A sixth grader adapted the idea of doubling to create his own story based on saving and spending money. The English language arts Standards call for children to "employ a wide range of strategies as they write" (NCTE/IRA 1996, p. 3). In these examples, children employed the strategy of adapting the structure of a story to create their own tales.

These Standards also propose that children generate ideas and questions, as well as pose their own problems. This notion was evident when third graders wondered how many gifts Emma must have received altogether and when sixth graders asked how many grains of rice were received in total. In both cases, children extended the text by posing questions that were not addressed in the story. In these various ways, the teachers and children of these classrooms used the strategy of problem posing to bring to life many of the aspects of these Standards for mathematics and language arts.

We conclude with a list of books that have some interesting problem-posing potential.

References

Some Good Books for Problem-Posing Extensions

Aker, Suzanne. *What Comes in 2's, 3's, and 4's?* Illus. Bernie Karlin. New York: Simon & Schuster, 1990.

Anno, Mitsumasa. *Anno's Magic Seeds.* New York: Philomel, 1995.

Appelt, Kathi. *Bats on Parade.* Illus. Melissa Sweet. New York: Morrow, 1999.

Birch, David. *The King's Chessboard.* Illus. Devis Grebu. New York: Dial, 1988.

Brown, Margaret Wise. *Four Fur Feet.* Illus. Remy Charlip. New York: Dell, 1961/1990.

Brown, Ruth. *Ten Seeds.* New York: Knopf, 2001.

Crews, Donald. *Ten Black Dots.* New York: Greenwillow Books, 1986.

Cuyler, Margery. *100th Day Worries.* Illus. Arthur Howard. New York: Simon & Schuster, 2000.

Dee, Ruby, reteller. *Two Ways to Count to Ten: A Liberian Folktale.* Illus. Susan Meddaugh. New York: Henry Holt, 1988.

Dodds, Dayle Ann. *The Great Divide.* Illus. Tracy Mitchell. Cambridge, MA: Candlewick Press, 1999.

Enzensberger, Hans Magnus. *The Number Devil: A Mathematical Adventure.* Illus. Rotraut Susanne Berner. Trans. Michael Henry Heim. New York: Henry Holt, 2000.

Franco, Betsy. *Grandpa's Quilt.* Illus. Linda A. Bild. New York: Children's Press, 1999.

Friedman, Aileen. *The King's Commissioners.* Illus. Susan Guevara. New York: Scholastic, 1994.

Giganti, Paul Jr. *Each Orange Had 8 Slices: A Counting Book.* Illus. Donald Crews. New York: Greenwillow, 1992.

———. *How Many Snails? A Counting Book.* Illus. Donald Crews. New York: Greenwillow, 1988.

Guettier, Bénédicte. *The Father Who Had 10 Children.* New York: Dial, 1999.

Hamm, Diane Johnston. *How Many Feet in the Bed?* Illus. Kate Salley Palmer. New York: Simon & Schuster, 1991.

Harris, Trudy. *Pattern Fish.* Illus. Anne Canevari Green. Brookfield, CT: Millbrook Press, 2000.

Harshman, Marc. *Only One.* Illus. Barbara Garrison. New York: Cobblehill Books/Dutton, 1993.

Hendra, Sue. *Numbers.* Cambridge, MA: Candlewick Press, 1999.

Hoban, Tana. *Let's Count.* New York: Greenwillow Books, 1999.

———. *26 Letters and 99 Cents.* New York: Scholastic, 1988.

Hong, Lily Toy, reteller. *Two of Everything: A Chinese Folktale.* Morton Grove, IL: Albert Whitman, 1992.

Hulme, Joy N. *Sea Squares.* Illus. Carol Schwartz. New York: Hyperion, 1991.

Hutchins, Pat. *The Doorbell Rang.* New York: Greenwillow Books, 1986.

Jenkins, Emily. *Five Creatures.* Illus. Tomek Bogacki. New York: Frances Foster Books, 2001.

Jocelyn, Marthe. *Hannah's Collections.* New York: Dutton, 2000.

Lesser, Carolyn. *Spots: Counting Creatures from Sky to Sea.* Illus. Laura Regan. San Diego: Harcourt Brace, 1999.

MacDonald, Suse. *Look Whooo's Counting.* New York: Scholastic, 2000.

Mathews, Louise. *Gator Pie.* Illus. Jeni Bassett. Littleton, MA: Sundance, 1995.

Merriam, Eve. *12 Ways to Get to 11.* Illus. Bernie Karlin. New York: Simon & Schuster, 1993.

Miller, Virginia. *Ten Red Apples: A Bartholomew Bear Counting Book.* Cambridge, MA: Candlewick Press, 2002.

Napoli, Donna Jo, and Richard Tchen. *How Hungry Are You?* Illus. Amy Walrod. New York: Atheneum, 2001.

Nozaki, Akihiro. *Anno's Hat Tricks.* Illus. Mitsumasa Anno. New York: Philomel, 1985.

Pinczes, Elinor J. *One Hundred Hungry Ants.* Illus. Bonnie MacKain. Boston: Houghton Mifflin, 1993.

———. *A Remainder of One.* Illus. Bonnie MacKain. Boston: Houghton Mifflin, 1995.

Pittman, Helena Clare. *A Grain of Rice.* New York: Bantam Skylark, 1986.

Sayre, April Pulley, and Jeff Sayre. *One Is a Snail, Ten Is a Crab.* Illus. Randy Cecil. Cambridge, MA: Candlewick Press, 2003.

Schwartz, David M. *How Much Is a Million?* Illus. Steven Kellogg. New York: Lothrop, Lee & Shepard, 1985.

———. *If You Hopped Like a Frog.* Illus. James Warhola. New York: Scholastic, 1999.

Sturges, Philemon. *Ten Flashing Fireflies.* Illus. Anna Vojtech. New York: North-South Books, 1995.

Tang, Greg. *The Grapes of Math: Mind-Stretching Math Riddles.* Illus. Harry Briggs. New York: Scholastic, 2001.

Tompert, Ann. *Grandfather Tang's Story.* Illus. Robert Andrew Parker. New York: Crown, 1990.

Trivas, Irene. *Emma's Christmas: An Old Song.* New York: Orchard Books, 1988.

Wells, Rosemary. *Emily's First 100 Days of School.* New York: Hyperion, 2000.

Zaslavsky, Claudia. *Number Sense and Nonsense: Building Math Creativity and Confidence through Number Play.* Chicago: Chicago Review Press, 2001.

Scholarly Works Cited

Brown, Stephen I., and Marion I. Walter. *The Art of Problem Posing.* Hillsdale, NJ: Lawrence Erlbaum, 1983/1990.

Dacey, Linda Schulman, and Rebeka Eston. *Growing Mathematical Ideas in Kindergarten.* Sausalito, CA: Math Solutions Publications, 1999.

Dewey, John. *Experience and Education.* New York: Macmillan, 1938.

National Council of Teachers of Mathematics. *Principles and Standards for School Mathematics.* Reston, VA: National Council of Teachers of Mathematics, 2000.

Schwartz, David M., and David J. Whitin. *The Magic of a Million: Activity Book.* New York: Scholastic, 1998.

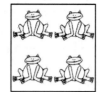

4

Using the Strategy of Book Pairs

In Chapter 3, we examined ways in which the strategy of problem posing opens up new avenues for mathematical and language arts discussions and explorations. Pairing books with a related theme, topic, concept, or other link is another way to encourage rich investigations. Here we show how teachers and children have extended this literary strategy of pairing to their mathematics classrooms. We also suggest additional titles to pair or to include in broader text sets or literature clusters. These stories and suggestions are intended to stir your imagination as you and your students read these pairs or to help you discover new text combinations yourselves. To this end, this chapter provides:

- A description of the pairing strategy and a discussion of the instructional purposes for employing the strategy from a literary perspective
- A discussion of ways to pair math-related books and benefits specific to the teaching and learning of mathematics
- Examples of the strategy in action, gathered from K–5 classrooms, covering a range of topics and genres
- Additional suggestions for book pairings
- Connections between the classroom examples and the Standards in language arts and mathematics

The Paired Books Strategy

You are probably familiar with the strategy of pairing or clustering related books into text sets for literary discussions and theme studies. There are many ways to pair books: by different genres, by different knowledge systems or content areas (e.g., a book about inventions and a book of historical fiction about the same time period), by different degrees of familiarity (e.g., one book that provides background knowledge for the second book), or by cultural perspectives, to name a few (Short and Harste 1996). Like problem posing, the strategy is based on the belief that optimal learning depends on opportunities to make meaningful connections between ideas and experience and to take and explore multiple points of view on a topic. In Short and Harste's words, "When readers read two or more texts that are related in some way, they are encouraged to share and extend their understandings of each text differently than if only one text had been read and discussed" (p. 537). Furthermore, when children engage in this strategy over time, they are likely to develop a habit of searching for connections on their own. The strategy provides many opportunities and benefits for literacy development:

1. *Encouraging rereading:* When books are intentionally paired and discussed, children have meaningful opportunities to revisit texts. Rereading develops fluency, which is especially important for ELL students and struggling readers. When rereading the first text of a pair, readers also discover that later interpretations are enhanced by the information from the reading of the second book.

2. *Examining author's craft:* Pairing, comparing, and contrasting books sharpen the reader's focus on the author's (and illustrator's) craft. For example, Author A did _____; Author B chose to do _____ instead. Children can study how an author's or an illustrator's style, choice of genre, and format set the mood and convey ideas or information. These explorations highlight the range of authoring possibilities and can inspire children to borrow techniques for their own writing (Fletcher 1996; Fletcher and Portalupi 1998; Portalupi and Fletcher 2001).

3. *Enhancing cross-curricular ties:* Using text sets and book pairs in literature studies can complement and extend work in social studies and science. Periods of history come alive through biography and historical fiction. The wonder of scientific facts is enhanced through poetry or photographic essays (Hancock 2000). This practice not only promotes meaningful learning, but it also allows for efficient use of time in today's busy classrooms.

Of course, in this book the most obvious cross-curricular tie is between mathematics and language arts. We now focus our attention on the specific topic of pairing math-related books.

Pairing Math-Related Books: Methods and Benefits

What are the particular benefits of pairing math-related books? The first is related to the idea of rereading mentioned previously. You probably have some students, perhaps second language learners, who feel more comfortable with mathematics than with reading. For these children, revisiting the texts to explore mathematical ideas can provide additional opportunities to read as well as look more closely at patterns and relationships.

It is also beneficial to study the author's and the illustrator's crafts from a mathematical standpoint. In Chapter 3, we discussed how questioning an author's intentions opened paths for mathematical explorations. Comparing and contrasting two or more books is another way to focus attention on mathematical authoring. Does the author, for example, use symbols (dots, cubes, numerals), charts, diagrams, or arrangements of objects to show numerical information? What relationships are highlighted by each choice? In the book *Counting Wildflowers* (1986), Bruce McMillan represents numbers in two ways. He photographed specific quantities of wild-flowers, and below each photo he includes a row of 10 dots (and later in the book, 20). For each quantity of flowers, the corresponding number of dots is colored in; the remaining dots are left blank. For 3 flowers, the circles look like this:

McMillan's choice invites children to explore combinations of addends that equal 10.

This unique treatment is a valuable one to pair with other counting books that represent number operations in different ways. Multiplication, for example, is represented by repeated addition in *Two Ways to Count to Ten* (Dee 1988) and by an array model in *One Hundred Hungry Ants* (Pinczes 1993). Discussions about books such as these can demonstrate that mathematical authoring decisions reflect a range of purposes and affect the readers' interpretations, just as literary decisions do.

Paired books can encourage students to describe and understand similarities and differences between related mathematical ideas. Each arithmetic and geometric progression, for example, has a unique pattern of growth. *If You Hopped Like a Frog* (Schwartz 1999) shows arithmetic progressions. If an average child could hop with the ability of a frog, the child could hop in 90-foot increments (90, 180, 270, etc.). Children can compare this constant rate with the geometric progression described in *One Grain of Rice* (Demi 1997). In the latter story, the given quantity, starting with 1, is doubled successively (1, 2, 4, 8, 16, 32, 64, etc.), thus growing much more dramatically.

Examples of the Paired Books Strategy in K–5 Classrooms

The benefits just discussed suggest some ways for teachers to choose book pairs: to demonstrate differing forms of representation or models, or to contrast related mathematical ideas. The classroom examples that follow demonstrate these and other ways to pair books:

- Pairing to explore our multicultural heritage (grade 5)
- Pairing by the same author (grade 1)
- Exploring geometry through book pairs (K)
- Pairing books about large numbers (grade 5)
- Investigating patterns in polygons (grade 3)

Connecting the Concept of Time with Students' Cultural Heritage

Book Pair: Anno, Mitsumasa. *All in a Day*. Illus. Raymond Briggs et al. New York: Philomel, 1986.

Singer, Marilyn. *Nine o'Clock Lullaby*. Illus. Frané Lessac. New York: HarperCollins, 1991.

Fifth-grade teacher Joy Wrigley wanted to select a book pair that she felt would be relevant to the rich cultural heritages of her students. Joy teaches a self-contained class of students in Brooklyn, New York; most of her students were born in countries outside the United States. She also wanted to select some books that incorporate a math concept that her students needed more help with, so she chose the concept of time. Many of her students had just learned to read a clock, and they needed practice determining elapsed time. These particular books focus on time and also raise some important scientific ideas about the rotation of the Earth and sun. For all these reasons, Joy selected two books that deal with time zones and the differences in time throughout the world.

Joy began the discussion by asking her students, "What time is it right now?" She then asked if it was the same time right now in Florida. What about California? Russia? Italy? Most of the students believed the time to be the same in all these places. Joy then read *All in a Day* to her students, as well as *Nine o'Clock Lullaby*. Both books include time zones in their stories. In the former book, the lives of nine children are all depicted on January 1: a child in Chicago rides a sled at 9:00 a.m.; a Brazilian child is playing on the beach at 6:00 p.m.; a child in Tokyo is asleep at midnight; and so on. Readers follow each of these children in increments of 3-hour periods for 21 hours. Children are seen enjoying such universal activities as playing games, celebrating with family, and preparing special meals. In the latter book, the author includes more specific cultural activities, such as 10:00 p.m. in Puerto Rico featuring "Papa playing congas, Tio his guitar," while at 11:00 a.m. in Japan, "Grandfather floats a tulip so the fish can greet the spring." The books complement each other and generated some interesting discussions. Anno's book sparked a lively talk about how time zones worked, while the Singer book prompted a sharing of the children's own cultural activities in their native lands.

Even after hearing both stories, the children were still puzzled about how time zones worked. When Joy asked, "Who would like to say something about the times in these stories?" the children raised questions about these differences in time and season. The questions eventually led to a discussion about the movement of the Earth and the sun, enhancing the students' scientific understanding of the reasons for seasons. This brief excerpt from the class conversation shows how these first questions arose:

Other Suggested Books about Time:

Chimp Math: Learning about Time from a Baby Chimpanzee (Nagda and Bickel 2002)

The Story of Clocks and Calendars: Marking a Millennium (Maestro 1999)

Telling Time with Big Mama Cat (Harper 1998)

Nor: How can it be different times at the same time?

Teacher: What do you mean by that?

Nor: Look at the picture of China. It says it's 8 a.m. on January 1. In the picture of Australia it's 11 a.m. and it looks like it's summer.

Billy: Why do you think it's summer?

Carol: Well, the trees have leaves on them.

Shaza: The windows of the car are rolled down. What is that on top of the car?

Lori: Oh, it looks like a boat or canoe. Yeah, people use them when it's hot outside.

Katie: But how can it be summer if it's January? Hey, we found a mistake in the book!

Joy was particularly interested in this last comment since the children had found a few mistakes in some of their author study books (e.g., an inadvertent switching of proper names or an illustration that did not quite match all the details of a story). As literate readers do, they were trying to make sense of this puzzling situation and drew on previous experiences with texts to explain what they were reading. As Joy encouraged them to look at more of the pictures, however, they saw again how many different seasons were represented:

Nathali: Ah, so there really are many times in the world. The author couldn't have made that many mistakes.

Anna: What I don't get is how the seasons change. How can a few hours make a difference in the seasons?

Teacher: Why don't we bring that question to the floor? Any ideas?

Nick: Does it have something to do with the sun?

Billy: Yeah, I know. The sun moves.

Lori: The sun does *not* move!

Nor: Well, it has to be that. What else could it be?

Teacher: What do the rest of you think?

Carol: Isn't the sun too heavy to move?

German: What else could it be?

Billy: It's the Earth! The Earth is moving. That has to be it.

Nick: Billy is definitely right. I remember now. I read about this in a book. But the pictures [in *All in a Day*] make it seem more real. I guess that's why I didn't get it at first.

Nick's comment underscores the importance of representing mathematical concepts in different ways. Although Nick had an intuitive understanding of time zones from reading one book, he was still confused by Anno's book because the illustrations made the situation more real, more believable.

The class conversation about the rotation of the Earth around the sun prompted Rimon, who had just arrived from Bangladesh, to share some of his personal knowledge. He wanted to show his classmates what he had learned about the difference between night and day. He placed the edge of a textbook on the floor, showing the "dark" (down facing) side and the "light" (up facing) side to the class. He explained: "My teacher show me in my country. The book is the Earth. Light side is where sun is. Dark side is night time." The class was fascinated by Rimon's demonstration. His example prompted a further discussion, involving the globe, about how the Earth tilts on its axis and how the angle of the rays of the sun affect seasons around the world.

Many of the children thought the illustrations in *All in a Day* depicted the change in seasons more clearly than those in *Nine o'Clock Lullaby*. Perhaps that is why the discussion about time zones emerged from looking closely at Anno's book. The children were intrigued with *Nine o'Clock Lullaby* for different reasons. They noted that this book is constructed in a circular way—i.e., it begins and finishes in the same place. Of course, this fact was especially appealing to them since the story's setting is Brooklyn, their own home! They also enjoyed the particular activities for each culture described in the book. This aspect of the book encouraged them to talk about the kinds of activities they used to do in their former homelands. They also enjoyed finding the time differences between the countries mentioned in *Nine o'Clock Lullaby* and then locating these countries on the map or globe. Joy used these discussions to plan an extension activity. She invited the children to research the time difference between New York and their native lands. They were then to describe what they would be doing in each of these places. Thus, the experience gave the students practice in adding times—e.g., what is 6 hours later than New York time?—as well as the opportunity to share memories of their native lands.

Melissa calculated that Syria was a 7-hour time difference from New York. She drew a picture of her favorite activities: drinking tea, eating sunflower seeds, and "having a laughter" (Figure 4.1). She then calculated differences in time between New York and Syria and described her appropriate activities in each. She began, for instance, with 7 a.m. in New York (eating) and then had to add 7 hours to determine the time in Syria. She knew 5 more hours would equal 12:00 noon, so she added 2 more hours to reach 2 p.m. in Syria (at which time she would be playing outside with her brothers and sisters). The children began to use 12 o'clock as a benchmark for their adding.

Figure 4.1
Melissa Reflects Her Cultural
Background as She
Calculates the Time in
Her Homeland

Some of the children wanted to write their message in their native language, and Joy encouraged them to do so. In this way, they extended the book pairs by including a different facet of their culture. Tatiana wrote her response in Russian (Figure 4.2) as she depicted herself getting ready for bed. Daniela found it difficult to write about Albania because, she confessed quietly to Joy, "there's nothing left" to remember due to the many years of war. But she decided to draw a picture of herself playing (Figure 4.3) and said, "This is what I dream it to be."

This particular book pair enabled a class of fifth-grade students to discuss parts of their cultural heritage, practice calculating differences in time, and learn about the reasons for the range of times and seasons throughout the world. This book pair was clearly an interdisciplinary venture as students connected aspects of their personal lives with concepts in science and mathematics.

Pairing Books by the Same Author

Book Pair: Giganti, Paul Jr. *How Many Snails? A Counting Book.* Illus. Donald Crews. New York: Greenwillow Books, 1988.

Giganti, Paul Jr. *Each Orange Had 8 Slices: A Counting Book.* Illus. Donald Crews. New York: Greenwillow Books, 1992.

First-grade teacher Marci Weiss decided to share two books by Paul Giganti Jr. with her students for several reasons. Both stories use a

Figure 4.2
Tatiana Writes Her
Calculations in Both
English and Russian

Figure 4.3
Daniela Imagines 6:00 p.m.
as She Wishes It to Be in
Her Homeland

predictable linguistic structure that would support her emergent readers: "I went walking to the ____ and I wondered ____ . . ." and "On my way to the ____ . . ." Both stories use a pattern of three questions as another predictable feature. At the beginning of *How Many Snails?*, for instance, readers are presented with a picture of flowers in a field and asked, "How many flowers are there? How many flowers are yellow? How many flowers are yellow with black centers?" In *Each Orange Had 8 Slices*, readers are presented with 3 flowers, each with 8 petals, each petal with 2 black bugs. The questions posed are: "How many flowers are there? How many petals are there? How many black bugs are there in all?" Marci enjoyed the questions because they invite readers to interact with the text in an appealing way. She also noted that the books incorporate mathematical ideas that are important for her students to explore, such as classification, counting in sequence, and repeated addition. Thus, Marci had both literary and mathematical reasons for sharing these books with her students.

Since both stories involve looking at the attributes of objects, Marci decided to do the classification activity "What's My Rule?" with her students before reading the stories. She wanted to give her students a brief introduction to the concept of a set. First she placed a hula-hoop in the middle of the floor and asked her students to sit around it. She asked each student to take off one shoe and put it in the circle. Then she began taking out certain shoes from the circle and challenged the children to guess her rule for doing so. She played the game several times using such attributes as brown, heels, or sneakers. Marci felt this activity was a useful prelude to reading the books.

Marci then read *How Many Snails?* One of the first insights Marci had was that her students were counting in different ways to answer the questions. On the page with the flowers, Sandra said, she found that there were 15 flowers altogether by counting by 1s. Jasmine shared another way: "Well, I got 15 too, but I added 7 flowers on one page and 8 on the other." Joshua was amazed and remarked, "Oh yeah, look at that!" This interchange may have encouraged others to share their different ways of counting. When Chidi answered the next question, "There are 9 yellow flowers and 8 of them have black centers," Marci asked her to explain her counting strategy. She replied, "I first counted by 1s to find all the yellow ones, and then I saw 4 [with black centers] on one page and 4 on the other page, and I added to get 8." Both of these stories by Giganti have the potential to encourage counting in different ways, and teachers hold the key to whether that potential is realized. Marci supported these various counting strategies by asking questions about the process, such as "How did you get your answer? Did anyone count a different way?"

Other Books That Invite Children to Classify:

Five Creatures (Jenkins 2001)

Hannah's Collections (Jocelyn 2000)

A String of Beads (Reid 1997)

As the discussion continued, the students noted some of the linguistic attributes of the story. Danny asked, "Why does the author keep asking three questions?" (They returned to this question later when they heard the second story.) Juan asked, "What does the word *wonder* mean?" Sandra answered, "It means to think about something." Emian then directed the conversation to a mathematical aspect of the story: "Look, each time we get an answer, the number goes down." Again, Marci pushed the mathematical thinking of her students by asking, "Why do you suppose that is happening?"

Jasmine: Maybe because the author keeps adding on things to the questions.

Akeem: Look at the page with the dogs. First the author asks how many dogs, then how many have spots, then how many have spots and have their tongues hanging out.

Michael: He keeps saying "and" in the last question.

Anthony: Every question asks more stuff.

Esma: The number of stuff keeps going down and down because less and less stuff fits in.

Christopher: I don't understand!

Ashley: Look! Count the dogs first. There are 15. Then count the dogs that have spots. There are 4. Then count the dogs with spots and their tongues hanging out. There are 3. (She points to the objects on the page as she explains this reasoning to Christopher.)

Michael: There are less and less dogs that fit in.

Nakia: It's like different groups.

Deondre: First we start with a big group, and then it goes to a smaller group.

Laura: Every time we ask more stuff, the number goes down.

Sandra: That's like what we did with the hula-hoop.

In their own language, the children were explaining the inverse relationship of sets within a set: the more attributes listed, the fewer elements in the set.

As the story concluded, Marci asked if the children wanted to say anything else about the book. They offered other literary insights about the story:

David: Each page starts the same.

Akeem: He keeps starting with "I went walking" and "I wondered."

Diane: The author is repeating the same things over and over again.

Emian: Why would the author do that?

Nakia: Maybe so we will not forget the story.

Romario: Every question asks how many there are of something.

David: We always have to count to get an answer.

Hector: This book was showing different things, and not just snails.

The children's comments focused on the author's craft. They recognized the author's repetitive language and his use of three questions to frame the story. They carried over these insights to the next day when Marci read aloud the next Giganti story, *Each Orange Had 8 Slices.*

After reading the first pages, Joshua made the first connection: "There are three questions here too!" Nakia elaborated, "Oh, look. The questions look the same [more attributes are included in each successive question]." Juan said, "Both books keep asking how many." Even the teacher noticed a new connection between the two stories: the children were more likely to count-on by 2s, 3s, and 5s, rather than 1s, to find their answer. She wondered why this kind of counting was happening. As she looked more closely at this second story, she noticed that objects were already pregrouped for children to count, i.e., 2 bugs on each petal of a flower or 3 wheels on each tricycle. Some children still counted the total by 1s, but more of the class used the author's sets of objects as the basis for their counting. Thus, it was the children's comments that gave Marci a new perspective on these stories.

One of the most important mathematical insights about this second story was noted by Deondre: "The numbers [answers] keep going up." Jasmine added, "That's the opposite of the other book." David explained the reason for this increase to his classmates: "There are more things that fit into the answer." (For instance, there are 2 oranges, with 16 sections and 32 seeds altogether.) In this case, the original set (oranges) is multiplied by different attributes (sections and seeds), whereas in the first book the original set (the whole) was described in smaller subsets (parts). The stories highlight the difference between the multiplicative and additive properties of number. The children were noting this difference in their own language.

When Marci asked the children to compare the two books in other ways, they shared these insights:

Laura: The author keeps telling us what he sees [in both books].

Esma: Both books want us to find answers to questions.

Deondre: There are always three questions.

Sandra: In one the numbers go up and in the other the numbers go down.

Teacher: Why do you suppose the author wrote these books in the way that he did?

Diane: Maybe he wanted to make the math stuff fun for us kids.

Nakia: I think he likes colorful things and loves to ask a lot of questions.

Chidi: Maybe his favorite thing to do is count and he wanted to make books that want you to count and get an answer.

Suggested Authors and Illustrators to Study:

Mitsumasa Anno

Kathi Appelt

Tana Hoban

Bruce McMillan

David M. Schwartz

Robert E. Wells

The children were reflecting on the author's intentions and his use of mathematical questions to intrigue the reader and give the story a predictable format.

The next day Marci invited her students to create a story in the style of Giganti. All the children used the structure of *How Many Snails?* because it allowed them to work with smaller numbers. Many of the children also followed the patterned language of this book by writing, "I went walking to the _____ and I wondered _____." They also used familiar contexts. For instance, Niki described her dance school (Figure 4.4) and discussed why she chose this situation: "I always go to dance class and everyone but me has on a pink tutu. I want to be the dancer one day with the pink tutu." Denise used the familiar context of the grocery store/fruit stand to describe her favorite fruit of apples (Figure 4.5). When the children shared their stories, questions, and answers with the whole class, David remarked, "Look, all the numbers go down like the book." Jasmine added, "Yes, less and less stuff fit into the group." So the children used their own stories to connect with an important mathematical idea of the story.

In summary, this book pair allowed children to examine the author's craft of fashioning an intriguing story. It also allowed them to describe the comparison between the additive part-to-whole relationship and the multiplicative context of equal groups.

Pairing Books about Shapes in Our Environment

Book Pair: Feldman, Judy. *Shapes in Nature.* Chicago: Children's Press, 1991.

Johnson, Stephen T. *Alphabet City.* New York: Viking, 1995.

A kindergarten teacher planned to go on a shape hunt with her students, identifying shapes in their schoolyard (basic shape recognition was also part of the kindergarten curriculum). In preparation for this walk, she selected two books that invite readers to do some careful observing. In *Shapes in Nature*, the author uses photographs of scenes in nature and matching black outlines to help children pay attention to the shapes all around them. Ovals, circles, triangles, and squares are some of the featured shapes. One of the strengths of the book is that it represents a single shape in different ways; a triangle, for example, is shown as a mountaintop, a fish's fin, the teeth of a shark, and a melting piece of ice. In *Alphabet City*, readers are invited to find the shape of each letter of the alphabet hidden in paintings of

Figure 4.4
Niki's Story Based on
Giganti's *How Many Snails?*

Figure 4.5
Denise's Story Based on
Giganti's *How Many Snails?*

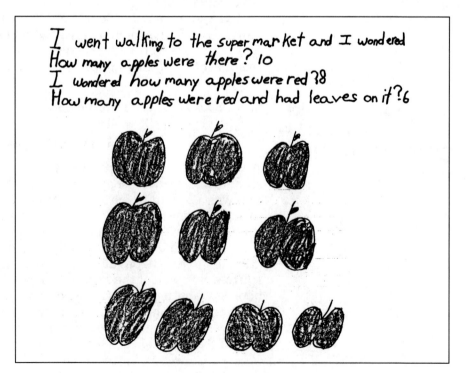

city life. We find an *A* in the sawhorses used by a construction worker, a *Y* in the repeating streetlights over a highway, and a *B* in the fire escape of an apartment building. The teacher, Melissa Sawicki, also found it interesting that one book focused on the natural world and the other looked at shapes in an urban setting.

She began by sharing *Shapes in Nature*. She decided, however, to cover up the black silhouette of a shape (at the top of the page) with a sticky note so that the class wouldn't know what shape they were supposed to be looking for. Instead, she wanted them to notice many different things and not be confined to a particular kind of response. As Melissa shared the picture of four robin eggs in a nest, she posed an open-ended question: "What do you notice about this picture?" The children's responses included "a nest," "eggs," "blue eggs," and "ovals." The photograph of a starfish prompted "red star," "starfish shape," and "white circles" (the children noticed small white circles on the exterior of the starfish). At this point, one of the children asked, "What's under that piece of paper?" Melissa explained, "There is a picture of a shape to show us which shape the author saw in the photograph." When Melissa showed them the star shape for the starfish, a child said, "But there's only one! We found more!" Melissa reaffirmed their confidence by replying, "Yes, we are super shape detectives!"

Next she shared *Alphabet City*. The children immediately found the *A* shape in the sawhorses but did not stop with that observation. Since they were accustomed to finding shapes in the first book, they continued the shape hunt in the second book. In addition to the *A* shape, for instance, they also found triangles, ovals, arrows, and rectangles. Melissa had each student come to the front of the room and trace the shape so all could see the individual observation more clearly. Throughout the reading of this book, the children pointed out shapes as well as letters in the pictures. Their responses demonstrate one benefit of reading a pair of books: the reading of the first book influences the reading of the second book.

Once she had read both books to the children, Melissa asked them, "How are these two books the same?" Some of their responses included:

- They both have shapes in them.
- They're both in color.
- They have some shapes that are the same.
- Every place is made out of shapes. If you look at everything, there are always shapes.

This last comment led the class to identify many different shapes in their classroom. Melissa asked them what shape was most common, and they all agreed it was the rectangle. Next the children were asked to find differences between the two books, and they noted these distinctions:

- One book has ABCs and the other one doesn't.
- There are no heart shapes in the ABC book.
- One book has paintings and the other one has real pictures (photographs).
- The *Shapes in Nature* book has "not normal" shapes in it (irregular shapes).

All of the children's comments related to similarities and differences show some astute observations. They recognized that interesting shapes abound in many different contexts. They saw that shapes could be classified in different ways, such as letter shapes, regular shapes, and "not normal" shapes (by which they meant hearts, ovals, and spirals). These observations could lead to other classification experiences with additional shapes, such as pattern blocks or the 3-D GeoBlocks. It is interesting that they tied the two books together by saying that both were shape books. Melissa might have extended that idea by sharing additional shape books to see if the children noticed both shapes and letters in these other books.

At the end of this conversation about similarities and differences, one child connected the two books in still another way: "Hey, all the shapes and the letters are outside." This comment led nicely into Melissa's next invitation: to go on a shape hunt outside their school, take pictures of what they find, and assemble their observations into a class book. The children were eager to start! Melissa brought along her Polaroid camera and took pictures of what the children noticed, such as the parallelograms on the school window grating, the circles on the fire hydrant, and the pentagons on the iron gates. Michelle wrote about the "half circle" she found in the arches of the school windows (Figure 4.6). Melissa was pleased that the children were "recognizing smaller parts of bigger things." Looking closely at the details of objects was one of Melissa's goals for her students. Their shape book was certainly evidence that they were becoming observers of their world.

Other Books That Show Shapes in the Natural World:

Arlene Alda's ABC (Alda 1993)

Arlene Alda's 1 2 3 (Alda 1998)

The Butterfly Alphabet (Sandved 1996)

Echoes for the Eye: Poems to Celebrate Patterns in Nature (Esbensen 1996)

Look Book (Hoban 1997)

A Star in My Orange: Looking for Nature's Shapes (Rau 2002)

Pairing Books about Large Numbers

Book Pair: Anno, Masaichiro, and Mitsumasa Anno. *Anno's Mysterious Multiplying Jar.* Illus. Mitsumasa Anno. New York: Philomel, 1983.

Demi. *One Grain of Rice.* New York: Scholastic, 1997.

Eloise Eisenhardt chose to use this book pair with her fifth-grade son, Chris, as a way to explore similarities and differences between factorials (Anno and Anno) and doubling (Demi). Demi's book,

Figure 4.6
Students on a Shape Hunt
Identify Shapes in Their World

which we described in Chapter 1, is a retelling of the Indian tale in which a seemingly small reward of one grain of rice, doubled each day for 30 days, results in a selfish raja giving enough rice to feed the entire kingdom. Demi illustrates the growth through written descriptions as well as through illustrations, including triple and quadruple page foldouts that accentuate the progression. *Anno's Mysterious Multiplying Jar* is a puzzle book in which the reader is invited to explore how a magic jar containing successive quantities of objects (1 island, 2 countries, 3 mountains, etc., up to 10 new jars) results in the astonishing total of 3,628,800 new jars. The Annos follow the pictorial story with a series of arrays of dots demonstrating the rate of growth from 1! to 8! ($1 \times 2 \times 3 \times 4 \times 5 \times 6 \times 7 \times 8$). (The symbol ! is a mathematical sign for a factorial. A factorial is the product of a given series of consecutive whole numbers beginning with 1.) Even when the authors use tiny dots, the big pages cannot accommodate the arrays for 9! and 10! This fact alone highlights the extraordinary rate of growth that results from factorials. Eloise thought that the various forms of representation in each book worked well for comparing and contrasting each numerical pattern.

Chris's initial responses to the two books reflected the genre of each. When the story reached day 16 in *One Grain of Rice,* Chris remarked, "The raja is getting nervous that his reward was too much." The plot, illustrations (the raja putting his hand to his chin in an anxious way), and mathematical sequence all worked together to create the suspenseful tone that captured Chris's interest. During the reading of the Annos' book, Chris remarked more on the mathematical pattern: "Factorials always have to be multiplied by all of the numbers below them," and "It must have taken him [the authors] a long time to draw his book so it would be just right." These comments demonstrate the potential of using this book pair to study an author's purpose: Demi's primary purpose is to entertain, while the Annos' is to inform.

Chris also compared the mathematical representations in the two books. He noticed, "The elephants carrying all the rice for Rani is like the dot page for 8! because they both show huge numbers of things." Comparing these two representations also reveals important differences. The Annos were able to represent the entire quantity (40,320) in their array, but the amount in Demi's book was far greater: 536,870,912 grains of rice. The solution—two double foldout pages showing 256 elephants carrying bags of rice—is somewhat like a pictograph. Although the students did not pursue this idea, closer examination could have led to investigations of additional ways to represent large quantities, including exponential notation.

Another of Chris's comments led to a closer examination of the two number sequences. In contrasting the two books, he said that the Annos' book was "more complicated." Eloise asked Chris to explain, and he continued, "With factorials you have to remember all the things that come before, and with doubling you just multiply by two all the time." By describing the sequences in his own words, Chris demonstrated his understanding of each.

Finally, Eloise asked Chris to create two stories of his own. Since Halloween was approaching, Chris immediately thought that rather than focusing on rice, huge quantities of candy would be exciting. To ensure mathematical accuracy, he referred to a chart that Demi includes at the end of her book. He called his story "Halloween Dream—A Doubling Story."

> One Halloween I had a dream that I went to 20 houses to trick-or-treat. The first house I went to gave me only one piece of candy, which I thought was a "rip off!" The second gave me two pieces, a Snickers and a Skittles. The third gave me four, the fourth gave me eight, the fifth gave me 16, and the sixth gave me 32. I noticed that

every house I went to gave me double from the house before! By the time I got to house number twenty, they gave me 524,288 pieces. I figured out I had 1,048,576 pieces of candy. I had to use my red wagon, a wheelbarrow, and a Mack truck to get it all home. I figured I could eat about 500 pieces before blowing up. The truck dumped the candy out on my front lawn. I called all my friends and we feasted for years.

Like Demi, Chris embedded the numerical sequence in a logical story line. He chose to show the sequence in detail in the first paragraph and name the sequence (doubling) to be clear to his audience. In the second paragraph, he, like Demi, skipped ahead to keep the story moving. Chris's own voice shines through the story in his own style of exaggeration (my red wagon, a wheelbarrow, and a Mack truck) and humor.

Chris continued the Halloween theme by writing "Halloween Factorials." Again he followed the author's structural demonstration, this time drawing successive pictures and labeling each with numerical information: One town, with 2 blocks, with 3 houses on each block, with 4 bowls of candy in each house, with 5 pieces of candy in each bowl, yielding 120 pieces of candy (Figure 4.7). Like the Annos, Chris made the idea of factorials clear without developing a plot. In the afterword of their book, the Annos also apply factorials to everyday life, such as calculating all possible seating arrangements. Building on this cue, Eloise asked Chris to extend his story as well. Chris chose to tie his application directly to his candy theme (Figure 4.8). He retrieved 4 pieces of candy from his trick-or-treat bag and labeled a piece of paper: "$4! = 4 \times 3 \times 2 \times 1 = 24$." Commenting, "I can eat these in 24 different ways," he numbered the page from 1 to 24. Together Chris and Eloise worked to record all the possible orders of consumption (ending, of course, with consuming the candy in Chris's favorite order, which he starred on his page). Certainly this activity helped Chris to better understand and appreciate properties of the factorial sequence, as well as to experiment with forms of representation that correspond with authoring purposes.

Eloise chose one more experience with this book pair, this time to contrast the two mathematical patterns. She asked Chris to examine the two books once again in order to compare the two ways of multiplying. Chris answered, "They're different. I think factorials grow faster." Eloise noticed that Chris phrased his comment a bit tentatively, so she therefore (wisely!) asked him to explain his think-

> **Other Books That Explore Large Numbers:**
>
> *If the World Were a Village* (Smith 2002)
>
> *Incredible Comparisons* (Ash 1996)
>
> *In the Next Three Seconds* (Morgan 1999)
>
> *Is a Blue Whale the Biggest Thing There Is?* (Wells 1993)
>
> *On Beyond a Million* (Schwartz 1999)
>
> *One Million* (Hertzberg 1993)
>
> *What's Faster Than a Speeding Cheetah?* (Wells 1997)

ing. "If I doubled 100 it would be 200, but if I figured out 100! it would be a lot more," he replied. Eloise then suggested that Chris test his hypothesis with a simplified problem to make the calculations manageable. Chris chose 4!, that is, $4 \times 3 \times 2 \times 1 = 24$, compared with four doublings, 1, 2, 4, 8, <u>16</u>, thus confirming his hypothesis. When she reflected on this part of the experience, Eloise commented, "The books had given him the idea and pictures of these concepts. Having read the books, he was able to make an educated guess based on his newly acquired knowledge which he proved to be correct."

Through careful examination of both books, Chris was able to appreciate the unique properties of each mathematical sequence. He considered different forms of representation, such as the Annos' arrays and Demi's foldout pages. His original writing demonstrated his knowledge of literary elements and the match between format and purpose. Finally, relating these mathematical ideas to his own experiences and through his personal form of humor gave Chris an important sense of ownership.

Pairing Books about Patterns in Polygons

Book Pair: Burns, Marilyn. *The Greedy Triangle.* Illus. Gordon Silveria. New York: Scholastic, 1994.

Friedman, Aileen. *A Cloak for the Dreamer.* Illus. Kim Howard. New York: Scholastic, 1994.

Figure 4.7
Chris's Halloween-Themed
Factorial Story

At Raemala Dookan's school, third graders are expected to be able to compare and contrast polygons in different ways, and Raemala felt that this book pair would encourage that kind of exploration. In conjunction with *The Greedy Triangle,* she asked the children to draw the diagonals of polygons to make triangles. She then used her students' insight about fitting together triangles as a way for them to explore how triangles tessellate, or cover, a plane (based on *A Cloak for the Dreamer*). Thus, Raemala used the first story and an extension activity as a bridge to the second story.

In *The Greedy Triangle,* a seemingly happy triangle lives a busy life supporting bridges, catching the wind for sails, acting as a slice of pie, and much more. But it soon gets tired of doing these same old things and imagines that if it had one more side, and one more

Figure 4.8
Chris's Extension of His
Halloween Factorial Story

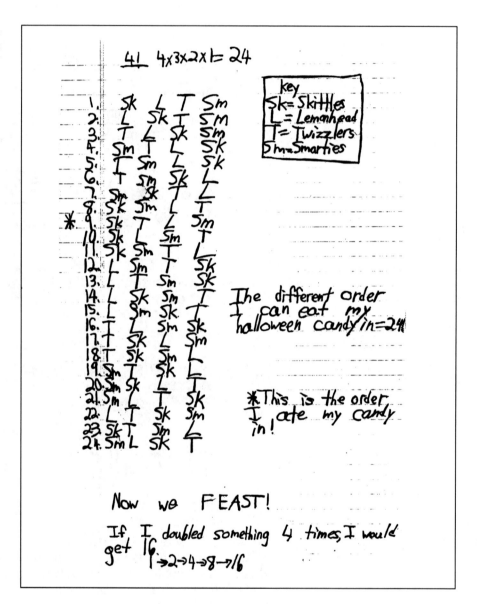

angle, life would be far more interesting. The local shapeshifter complies with the request, and the triangle becomes a quadrilateral. Yet the shape is not happy for long being a quadrilateral, or for that matter a pentagon, or a hexagon. In fact, it finally adds so many sides that it doesn't know which end is up! It returns to being a triangle, content to do all the things it had enjoyed doing from the very beginning.

In *A Cloak for the Dreamer*, shapes also play a key role in the story. A tailor has three fine sons whom he enlists to help him make warm cloaks for the archduke. Two of the sons use shapes that fit together without any gaps, such as rectangles, squares, and triangles. The third son wants to travel and see the world and has little interest in being a tailor. He makes a cloak out of circles, which has many gaps in it. But eventually the circles are cut and trimmed into hexagons, which do fit together. This new cloak is given to the third son as a gift so that he can stay warm as he sets out to see the world.

Raemala felt that the first story would generate discussion about polygons, and it certainly did. Students had learned some of the names of basic shapes, and they were trying to predict which shape would come next in the story. When the triangle became a quadrilateral, some of the students were surprised. The following conversation ensued:

> *Jordy:* I thought it would become a square.
>
> *Joanna:* I thought it would become a rectangle.
>
> *Teacher:* What is a quadrilateral?
>
> *Nusrat:* It could have something to do with 4 sides. I know *bi* means "two," and *tri* means "three," and *quad* means "four."
>
> *Teacher:* Can anyone think of some quadrilaterals?
>
> *Michael:* I know squares and rectangles have 4 sides.
>
> *Nusrat:* A diamond . . . I mean a rhombus has 4 sides.
>
> *Teacher:* Is a square always a quadrilateral?
>
> *Jordy:* A quadrilateral is any 4-sided shape, and a square has 4 sides, so it has to be.
>
> *Teacher:* Does a quadrilateral always have to be a square?
>
> *Ronald:* No, there are other 4-sided shapes, like trapezoids, rectangles, and a rhombus.

The Greedy Triangle provided a meaningful context for discussing the attributes of polygons. The children's interest in language continued when they were surprised that a 5-sided shape did not begin with *cinq*. They had been writing cinquains recently and they knew *cinq* meant "five."

When the children discussed the entire story at the end of the reading, several students commented on this changing polygon shape. Jordy said, "As you add more sides and more angles, the shapes look more and more round." Ronald agreed: "I always thought that circles had no angles or sides, but maybe they have so many that we just can't see them." Joanna replied, "Yeah, maybe it's too many to count." Nusrat surmised even further, "Oh, wow, circles have an infinity amount of sides and angles."

Figure 4.9
Noel Identifies the Triangles within a Trapezoid and a Pentagon

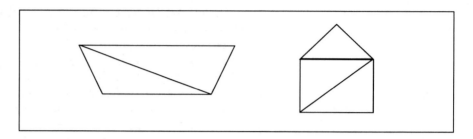

Next, Noel used her knowledge of geometry to interpret the triangle's actions: "I don't know why the triangle wanted to become other shapes. It was better just staying a triangle because all those other shapes it turned into were really made from triangles." Raemala asked her to come to the chalkboard to draw what she meant. Noel drew a trapezoid and a pentagon and then used diagonals to make triangles within them (Figure 4.9).

Noel's comment made an interesting literary as well as mathematical point. The triangle didn't need to become something else, because even though it appeared to be different, it was still carrying about parts of its original self. Also, Noel's geometric observation opened up an investigation into the number of diagonals and triangles in successively larger polygons. Raemala challenged the children to pursue this idea further, and they found the following pattern:

Number of Sides	Number of Diagonals	Number of Triangles Formed
3	0	1
4	1	2
5	2	3
6	3	4
7	4	5
8	5	6

The children described these patterns in several ways:

- The shapes get more sides as they get more triangles.
- There are 2 fewer triangles than the number of sides in the shape.
- There are 2 more sides in the shape than the number of triangles that make it up.
- The number of triangles goes up as the number of sides gets bigger.
- There are 3 fewer diagonals than the number of sides.
- The number of triangles is always 1 more than the number of diagonals.

Figure 4.10
Tessellations

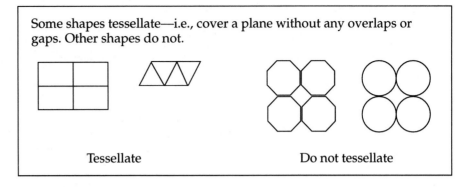

As Raemala prepared to read *A Cloak for the Dreamer,* she wanted to build on what the students had learned from this first experience. Since the first story focused primarily on triangles and the second story focused on the concept of tessellations, Raemala decided to combine these two ideas. Before reading the second story, she gave the children several circles, triangles, squares, rectangles, and hexagons and challenged them to see which shapes would fit together without any spaces in between them. They found that only the circles left gaps. Some of the children predicted that any polygon (except the circle) could tessellate since it could be divided into triangles (as they had learned from the first experience). The students hypothesized that if triangles by themselves could tessellate, then any polygon could also. Raemala intended to give the children more time to test out this idea on another day. Although this hypothesis would not be proved (see Figure 4.10), Raemala was pleased that the children were trying to make connections to what they had been learning. The paired stories provided the catalyst for this kind of thinking.

After hearing *The Cloak of the Dreamer,* the children compared the two stories. Michael commented that "both stories talk about where we can find different shapes in the world." Just as shapes are everywhere, so are tessellations such as bricks, tiles, and the honeycombs on beehives. Joanna argued that both stories featured main characters with the same inner conflict—i.e., being unhappy with their current situation: "Misha [the dreamer] was not going to be happy unless he explored the world, and the triangle wouldn't have known he was happy being a triangle if he didn't become other shapes first. They both did what made them happy in the end." She felt that both characters were true to themselves; they both had dreams and they followed them. In summary, the children made numerous literary and mathematical connections between the two stories.

Figure 4.11
Book Pairing Variations

> Pairing one book with different alternatives can highlight a range of mathematical ideas:
>
> *A Remainder of One* (Pinczes 1995), **paired with these books:**
>
> *The Great Divide* (Dodds 1999)   *Bats on Parade* (Appelt 1999)
> **Highlights divisibility of**   **Highlights square numbers**
> **numbers**
>
> *One Hundred Hungry Ants* (Pinczes 1993)
> **Highlights factors of a number**

A Medley of Other Book Pairs to Explore

Following are some other possible book pairs for you to explore. We've listed brief descriptors of each to spark your and your students' imaginations. Chapter 5 includes more detailed annotations for some of these books. Note also that some books pair well with many different books and that different pairings are likely to result in different classroom investigations (Figure 4.11).

Adler, David A. *America's Champion Swimmer: Gertrude Ederle.* Illus. Terry Widener. San Diego: Harcourt, 2000.
- Biography of first woman to swim the English Channel
- Real-life applications of time, distance, rate

Brown, Don. *Alice Ramsey's Grand Adventure.* Boston: Houghton Mifflin, 1997.
- Fictionalized account of first woman to cross the United States by car
- Real-life applications of time, distance, rate

Appelt, Kathi. *Bats on Parade.* Illus. Melissa Sweet. New York: Morrow, 1999.
- Story told in verse
- Shows square formations in arrays, 1–10, in visual and symbolic representations

Ross, Catherine Sheldrick. *Squares: Shapes in Math, Science and Nature.* Illus. Bill Slavin. Toronto: Kids Can Press, 1996.
- Activity and resource book
- Gives historical and cultural information; shows functions, uses, and properties of squares

Ash, Russell. *The World in One Day*. New York: DK, 1997.
- Wide range of global statistics
- Informational resource book

Smith, David. *If the World Were a Village: A Book about the World's People*. Illus. Shelagh Armstrong. Toronto: Kids Can Press, 2002.
- Statistics about world population
- Based on ratio of world village as 100 people
- Raises ethical issues

Baranski, Joan Sullivan. *Round Is a Pancake*. Illus. Yu-Mei Han. New York: Dutton, 2001.
- Predictable rhyme; imaginary medieval setting
- Circles, spheres, cylinders

Thong, Roseanne. *Round Is a Mooncake: A Book of Shapes*. Illus. Grace Lin. San Francisco: Chronicle Books, 2000.
- Predictable rhyme; Chinese American family; contemporary urban setting
- Circles, squares, and rectangles

Chinn, Karen. *Sam and the Lucky Money*. Illus. Cornelius Van Wright and Ying-Hwa Hu. New York: Lee & Low, 1995.
- Chinese American family; contemporary urban setting; theme of benevolent acts
- Money; saving and spending

Mollel, Tololwa M. *My Rows and Piles of Coins*. Illus. E. B. Lewis. New York: Clarion Books, 1999.
- Tanzanian family; family relationships; responsibility
- Money; saving and spending

Crosbie, Michael J., and Steve Rosenthal. *Architecture Shapes*. New York: Wiley, 1993.
- Photographs with labels
- Variety of shapes in architecture

Hoban, Tana. *So Many Circles, So Many Squares*. New York: Greenwillow Books, 1998.
- Photographs, no text
- Natural and manufactured objects; only circular and square shapes

Dodds, Dayle Ann. *The Great Divide.* Illus. Tracy Mitchell. Cambridge, MA: Candlewick Press, 1999.
- Fanciful, predictable story
- Successive halving of 80

Hong, Lily, reteller. *Two of Everything: A Chinese Folktale.* Morton Grove, IL: Albert Whitman, 1992.
- Humorous Chinese folktale
- Doubling numbers

Enzensberger, Hans Magnus. *The Number Devil: A Mathematical Adventure.* Illus. Rotraut Susanne Berner. New York: Henry Holt, 2000.
- Chapter book; dream setting
- Exploration of number patterns

Scieszka, Jon. *Math Curse.* Illus. Lane Smith. New York: Viking, 1995.
- Humorous picture book; school/home setting
- Mathematical view of the world

Fleischman, Paul. *Lost! A Story in String.* Illus. C. B. Mordan. New York: Holt, 2000.
- Storytelling with string figures; strong female protagonist
- Historical information and directions for making string figures included

Tompert, Ann. *Grandfather Tang's Story.* Illus. Robert Andrew Parker. New York: Crown, 1990.
- Storytelling with tangrams; Chinese setting
- Illustrations show how figures are made

Franco, Betsy. *Grandpa's Quilt.* Illus. Linda A. Bild. New York: Children's Press, 1999.
- Humorous story; African American intergenerational characters
- Arrays for 36
- Rearrangement of triangles as well as squares

Pinczes, Elinor J. *One Hundred Hungry Ants.* Illus. Bonnie MacKain. Boston: Houghton Mifflin, 1993.
- Humorous story told in verse
- Arrays for 100

Giganti, Paul Jr. *Each Orange Had 8 Slices: A Counting Book.*
Illus. Donald Crews. New York: Greenwillow Books, 1992.
  - Predictable structure; counting puzzle book
  - Invites repeated addition

Tang, Greg. *The Grapes of Math: Mind-Stretching Math Riddles.*
Illus. Harry Briggs. New York: Scholastic, 2001.
  - Addition riddles told in verse
  - Invites a variety of grouping strategies

Harris, Trudy. *Pattern Fish.* Illus. Anne Canevari Green.
Brookfield, CT: Millbrook Press, 2000.
  - Predictable format; humorous
  - Visual, aural, and movement patterns; multiple representations per page

Williams, Rozanne Lanczak. *Mr. Noisy's Book of Patterns.* Illus.
Kathleen Dunne. Cypress, CA: Creative Teaching Press, 1995.
  - Predictable format; humorous
  - Patterns in sound; one representation per page

Jenkins, Emily. *Five Creatures.* Illus. Tomek Bogacki. New York:
Frances Foster Books, 2001.
  - European American family and their pets
  - Classification of attributes of family members; a variety of arrangements

Johnson, Angela. *One of Three.* Illus. David Soman. New York:
Orchard Books, 1995.
  - African American family; sibling/parental relationships
  - Two examples of 1:3 relationship

Lankford, Mary D. *Dominoes around the World.* Illus. Karen
Dugan. New York: Morrow, 1998.
  - Picture book; multicultural
  - One material; many game variations around the world

Zaslavsky, Claudia. *Math Games & Activities from around the
World.* Chicago: Chicago Review Press, 1998.
  - Resource book; multicultural
  - Variety of games

Marshall, Janet. *Look Once, Look Twice.* New York: Ticknor &
Fields, 1995.

- Alphabet puzzle book; letter-shaped cutouts; realistic drawings
- Patterns in the natural world

Rotner, Shelley, and Richard Olivo. *Close, Closer, Closest.* New York: Atheneum, 1997.
- Sets of three photographs, close, closer, closest
- Patterns of color and texture of natural and manufactured objects

Nagda, Ann Whitehead, and Cindy Bickel. *Tiger Math: Learning to Graph from a Baby Tiger.* New York: Henry Holt, 2000.
- Nonfiction account of saving a baby tiger in a zoo setting; females in scientific/mathematical careers
- Several formats of graphs to record, convey, and analyze data

Wyatt, Valerie. *The Math Book for Girls and Other Beings Who Count.* Illus. Pat Cupples. Toronto: Kids Can Press, 2000.
- Activity resource book; showcases females in scientific/mathematical careers
- Wide range of mathematical topics

Rankin, Laura. *The Handmade Counting Book.* New York: Dial, 1998.
- Numbers represented in sign language

Zaslavsky, Claudia. *Count on Your Fingers African Style.* Illus. Wangechi Mutu. New York: Writers and Readers/Black Butterfly Books, 1999.
- Contemporary African setting; context of a marketplace to buy food
- Four African tribes use fingers in different ways to signify number

Schmandt-Besserat, Denise. *The History of Counting.* Illus. Michael Hays. New York: Morrow, 1999.
- Historical account of numeration systems

Zaslavsky, Claudia. *Number Sense and Nonsense: Building Math Creativity and Confidence through Number Play.* Chicago: Chicago Review Press, 2001.
- Activity resource book that includes numeration systems

Viewing These Experiences through Language and Mathematics Standards

The classroom stories recounted in this chapter demonstrate the enormous potential of investigating book pairs with children. Through this strategy of comparison and contrast, learners of all ages sharpen their mathematical and linguistic eyes and ears. It is through this process of looking closely that the children in these examples were able to make important connections, thereby expanding and deepening their knowledge and understanding.

Several English language arts Standards apply to all of the experiences described in this chapter: children "read a wide range of print and nonprint texts" (NCTE/IRA 1996, p. 3, Standard 1); they adjust their "spoken, written, and visual language" to communicate for different purposes (NCTE/IRA Standard 4); and they "participate as knowledgeable, reflective, creative, and critical members" of a community of learners (NCTE/IRA Standard 11). The fifth graders in our first anecdote expressed both their unique cultural identities and their shared identity (as residents of Brooklyn) through reading, writing, talking, and drawing. Through collaborative discussion, first graders discovered that a single author, Paul Giganti Jr., used a questioning format in two different books. Kindergarten children learning to look at objects and "parts of objects" became authors and photographers to capture features of their own school world. Chris, a fifth grader, showed his appreciation for two different genres, a traditional tale and a puzzle book, by creating two different texts with a similar Halloween theme. Third graders found that even stories about inanimate objects such as a triangle can convey a theme of self-acceptance and determination.

There are commonalities across all the anecdotes from the perspective of the NCTM Standards as well (NCTM 2000). Children use communication as "a way of sharing ideas and clarifying understanding" (NCTM Process Standards, Communication, p. 60); they "recognize and use connections among mathematical ideas" (p. 64) as well as apply mathematics in different contexts (NCTM Process Standards, Connections, p. 64); and they "create and use representations to organize, record, and communicate mathematical ideas" (NCTM Process Standards, Representation, p. 67). Through talking collaboratively and improvising models, a fifth-grade class connected the scientific context of the Earth's revolution and rotation to its mathematical application of temporal measurement. Both first graders and Chris made connections between mathematical ideas (investigating addition versus multiplication and different patterns using multiplication) and analyzed and created various representations (e.g., charts, stories, and pictures). Kindergartners and third graders discovered the functions and uses of geometric forms in the natural and built environments (shapes of objects; tessellations in bricks, tiles, and honeycombs). The kindergartners represented their new discoveries through photography and writing, while the third graders used manipulatives and diagrams.

We can also see other ties to specific mathematics and language arts Standards in each of the stories. By drawing on their various background experiences, fifth graders made sense of our system for measuring time and practiced calculations in meaningful contexts (NCTM Content Standards, Measurement). The first graders examined Giganti's authoring choices and sentence structure (NCTE/IRA Standard 3) while they differentiated between multiplicative and additive properties (NCTM Content Standards, Number and Operations and Algebra; Process Standards, Connections and Reasoning and Proof). The kindergartners, on their shape hunts in books and outdoors, conducted research through print and nonprint avenues (NCTE/IRA Standard 7) while they examined properties of geometric shapes and developed their sense of spatial relations (NCTM Content Standards, Geometry). Fifth grader Chris also investigated print and nonprint texts by comparing various representations for large numbers, such as verbal descriptions, arrays of dots, and pictures as symbols (NCTE/IRA Standard 6; NCTM Process Standards, Connections; Content Standards, Algebra). The third-grade children used their knowledge of prefixes (*bi-, tri-, quad-*) to comprehend a text and to make sense of appropriate mathematical vocabulary (NCTE/IRA Standard 3; NCTM Process Standards,

Communication). In each of these last two stories, children also offered conjectures (factorials increase at a faster rate than doubling; all polygons except circles can tessellate). In both cases, the children then tested and evaluated these conjectures (NCTE/IRA Standard 4; NCTM Process Standards, Reasoning and Proof).

We have shared this reflective analysis for two reasons. First, we wanted to demonstrate in yet one more way the rich potential of the book pairing strategy. Second, we hope to ignite in you a vision of new possibilities for you and your students. What new connections, investigations, and applications might you all find with these suggested pairs? What new pairs of books will you discover?

References

Children's Books Cited but Not Paired

Alda, Arlene. *Arlene Alda's ABC: What Do You See?* Berkeley, CA: Tricycle Press, 1993.

———. *Arlene Alda's 1 2 3: What Do You See?* Berkeley, CA: Tricycle Press, 1998.

Ash, Russell. *Incredible Comparisons.* New York: DK, 1996.

Dee, Ruby, reteller. *Two Ways to Count to Ten: A Liberian Folktale.* Illus. Susan Meddaugh. New York: Henry Holt, 1988.

Esbensen, Barbara Juster. *Echoes for the Eye: Poems to Celebrate Patterns in Nature.* Illus. Helen K. Davie. New York: HarperCollins, 1996.

Harper, Dan. *Telling Time with Big Mama Cat.* Illus. Barry Moser and Cara Moser. San Diego: Harcourt Brace, 1998.

Hertzberg, Hendrik. *One Million.* New York: Times Books, 1993.

Hoban, Tana. *Look Book.* New York: Greenwillow Books, 1997.

Jocelyn, Marthe. *Hannah's Collections.* New York: Dutton, 2000.

Maestro, Betsy. *The Story of Clocks and Calendars: Marking a Millennium.* Illus. Giulio Maestro. New York: Lothrop, Lee & Shepard, 1999.

McMillan, Bruce. *Counting Wildflowers.* New York: Lothrop, Lee & Shepard, 1986.

Morgan, Rowland. *In the Next Three Seconds.* Illus. Rod Josey and Kira Josey. New York: Puffin, 1999.

Nagda, Ann Whitehead, and Cindy Bickel. *Chimp Math: Learning about Time from a Baby Chimpanzee.* New York: Henry Holt, 2002.

Rau, Dana Meachen. *A Star in My Orange: Looking for Nature's Shapes.* Brookfield, CT: Millbrook Press, 2002.

Reid, Margarette S. *A String of Beads.* Illus. Ashley Wolff. New York: Dutton, 1997.

Sandved, Kjell B. *The Butterfly Alphabet.* New York: Scholastic, 1996.

Schwartz, David M. *If You Hopped Like a Frog.* Illus. James Warhola. New York: Scholastic, 1999.

———. *On beyond a Million: An Amazing Math Journey.* Illus. Paul Meisel. New York: Random House, 1999.

Wells, Robert E. *Is a Blue Whale the Biggest Thing There Is?* Morton Grove, IL: Albert Whitman, 1993.

———. *What's Faster Than a Speeding Cheetah?* Morton Grove, IL: Albert Whitman, 1997.

Scholarly Works Cited

Fletcher, Ralph. *A Writer's Notebook: Unlocking the Writer within You.* New York: Avon, 1996.

Fletcher, Ralph, and JoAnn Portalupi. *Craft Lessons: Teaching Writing K–8.* York, ME: Stenhouse, 1998.

Hancock, Marjorie R. *A Celebration of Literature and Response: Children, Books, and Teachers in K–8 Classrooms.* Upper Saddle River, NJ: Merrill, 2000.

Portalupi, Joann, and Ralph Fletcher. *Nonfiction Craft Lessons: Teaching Information Writing K–8.* York, ME: Stenhouse, 2001.

Short, Kathy G., and Jerome C. Harste, with Carolyn Burke. *Creating Classrooms for Authors and Inquirers,* 2nd ed. Portsmouth, NH: Heinemann, 1996.

5

Best Books for Exploring

This chapter contains an annotated list of books that are particularly good for exploring with children. In addition to books mentioned in previous chapters, we are featuring many other recent books as well as a few older ones that remain outstanding selections. Poetry books are listed separately at the end of Chapter 2. We have divided the following list of books into these categories:

- Introductory Counting Books
- Number Operations
- Informational Resource Books
- Measurement
- Geometry
- Classification

We have also used two symbols to classify the books even further:

M designates a multicultural dimension.

X designates interdisciplinary connections.

It is important that teachers of older children scan the titles of Introductory Counting Books to look for ones marked with an **X.** Although the counting sequence is fairly basic, these books do yield possibilities for interdisciplinary research into various social studies and science topics. Also, the category of Informational Resource Books contains numerous mathematical concepts such as measurement, geometry, and statistics.

Before we introduce these books to you, we want to share a few strategies for introducing these books to students. These strategies are meant to hook readers from the very beginning by soliciting their connections to a theme or topic and by providing an intriguing focus for listening. These ideas (along with one possible title for most) include:

1. Identify one of the main themes of the book and invite children to make some personal connections with that theme. For

instance, "One of the ideas this book discusses is sharing something equally. Before I read this book to you, let's talk with one another about some of the ways you share things with your family and friends." (*Two Greedy Bears,* Ginsburg)

2. Invite the children to listen for the problem in the story. For instance, "This story is about a man who had a serious problem. Listen for this problem and see what you think about how the problem could be solved. We'll talk about your ideas when the story is over." (*Grandpa's Quilt,* Franco)

3. Bring in an object that relates to the book. For instance, "I brought this scale to show you today because the story I'm going to read to you shows some people using a scale in their job. Listen to see how they use this scale. You might think about how their scale is the same and different from the scale that I have here." (*Tiger Math,* Nagda and Bickel)

4. Identify an unusual feature of the book, such as collage illustrations, or a dialogue, or its exclusive use of photographs. You might say to children, "This is a book that contains only photographs. There are no words. Why do you suppose someone would want to create a book that has only photographs? . . . Now let's look at the photographs together and talk about what we notice." (*So Many Circles, So Many Squares,* Hoban)

5. Invite the children to connect this book to others they might have read: "See if this book reminds you of any other book we have read together this year."

6. Invite children to compare and contrast the book with others they have read by the same author. You might say, "We have read several books by Anno already. What kinds of things does he write about? . . . Now let's listen to see how this book is the same and different from the other books he has written."

7. Involve children in a hands-on experience before introducing a book. When you do read the book, listen for connections the children might make. If such connections do not arise, ask directly, "How might this book be connected to the activity that we did yesterday with pattern blocks?" (*A Cloak for the Dreamer,* Friedman)

8. Select some information from the author's biographical statement to share with the students. Then suggest: "Let's look closely at how this information about the author is reflected in this book." (David M. Schwartz has a very appealing introduction to *If You Hopped Like a Frog* as he discusses his childhood imaginings about having the abilities of different animals.)

9. Relate the reasons that you chose this book: "This has always been a favorite book of mine because it reminds me of something that happened to me one time. See if it reminds you of anything in your life as I share it with you."

10. Relate how the book affected you the first time you read it: "The first time I read this book I couldn't believe how large a million, billion, and trillion really are. It really made me wonder about the large numbers that I hear people say all the time. See what you think about these large numbers as I read the story to you." (*How Much Is a Million?*, Schwartz)

Introductory Counting Books

Anderson, Lena. *Tea for Ten*. Trans. Elisabeth Kallick Dyssegaard. New York: R&S Books, 2000.

In this predictable 1 to 10 counting book, a series of animal visitors arrive at Hedgehog's home to enjoy friendship and food. The illustrations show the plus-one pattern as each new visitor enters and include subgroups for easier counting of the total party.

Anno, Mitsumasa. *Anno's Counting House*. New York: Philomel, 1982.

Readers see a set of 10 children move one by one from one house to another in this wordless text. A series of cutout windows gives glimpses of some of these children and encourages readers to predict which child will be moving next. It nicely highlights the part-to-whole relationship.

Bloom, Valerie. *Fruits: A Caribbean Counting Poem*. Illus. David Axtell. New York: Henry Holt, 1997. **(M, X)**

The cadence of Jamaican language, rich illustrations, and subtle humor about sibling relationships make this book a wonderful read-aloud choice. A glossary defines the tropical fruits and Jamaican words that appear in the text.

Bowen, Betsy. *Gathering: A Northwoods Counting Book*. Boston: Houghton Mifflin, 1999.

Older primary grade children will learn about details of seasonal activities in Minnesota's north woods. Younger children will enjoy finding and counting rhubarb pies, walleyes, and other objects (up to 12) illustrated through the beautiful woodblock prints.

Brown, Margaret Wise. *Four Fur Feet*. Illus. Remy Charlip. New York: Dell, 1961/1990.

All that readers can see of this furry animal is its four feet walking around the world and around the edges of each page. The predictable text and the intrigue of this mysterious creature make this book a favorite with young readers. Children often hypothesize who this creature might be.

Brown, Ruth. *Ten Seeds.* New York: Knopf, 2001. **(X)**

> This delightful subtraction story works wonderfully in a study of the plant cycle, the food chain, and gardening. A child plants ten sunflower seeds, which are reduced one by one under a variety of circumstances, only to be replaced when the one surviving plant produces a new supply.

Capucilli, Alyssa Satin. *Mrs. McTats and Her Houseful of Cats.* Illus. Joan Rankin. New York: Margaret K. McElderry Books, 2001.

> Mrs. McTats welcomes increasingly large groups of stray cats (and one puppy as a finale) into her home. The book is predictable through the repetitive story line, the increasing numbers of arriving cats (for most of the book), and alphabetically arranged names.

Cassie, Brian. *Say It Again.* Illus. David Mooney. Watertown, MA: Charlesbridge, 2000.

> Here is a book that introduces the concept of doubling in a very different way. It describes a variety of creatures from around the world whose names have a double sound. Some examples are the caracara (bird), chicochico (monkey), and molamola (fish). Endnotes give additional information on each creature and the probable origin of its name.

Cave, Kathryn. *One Child, One Seed: A South African Counting Book.* Photos. Giséle Wulfsohn. New York: Henry Holt, 2003. **(M, X)**

> Set in South Africa and illustrated with inviting color photographs, this counting book shows the process of planting, growing, and harvesting a meal. Informative sidebars tell more about the people of this village, including farm animals, games, and the roles of family members.

Cotten, Cynthia. *At the Edge of the Woods: A Counting Book.* Illus. Reg Cartwright. New York: Henry Holt, 2002.

> A variety of animals, birds, and insects (from 1 to 10) appears in the forest one morning. Illustrations are crisp and colorful, and groupings of creatures are easy to count. The rhyme scheme and repetition of certain phrases lend a predictable and appealing format to the text.

Crews, Donald. *Ten Black Dots.* New York: Greenwillow Books, 1986.

> Black dots highlight the round shapes of buttons, heads of toy soldiers, balloons, and other objects in this simple, rhymed

counting book. Different arrangements of the dots (in a row, in clusters, in two equal sets, etc.) invite children to share counting strategies.

Falwell, Cathryn. *Turtle Splash! Countdown at the Pond.* New York: Greenwillow Books, 2001.

Ten turtles are startled by noises in the forest, and they descend one by one from their log into the pond. The illustrations clearly show the separation of each turtle from the group, and observant readers will notice that each new "noisy" creature appears on the page before it actually disturbs the group. Instructions are included for making leaf prints similar to those in the book.

Freymann, Saxton, and Joost Elffers. *One Lonely Seahorse.* New York: Arthur A. Levine Books, 2000. **(X)**

This rhymed 1 to 10 counting book has an especially clever twist: all of the sea creatures and plants are composed of fruits, vegetables, and other produce. Different groupings on each page create opportunities for children to examine efficient ways to count.

Girnis, Margaret. *1 2 3 for You and Me.* Photos. Shirley Leamon Green. Morton Grove, IL: Albert Whitman, 2001.

Each number from 1 to 20 features a photograph of a child with Down syndrome and the corresponding number of balloons, cupcakes, dogs, baskets, and other easy-to-count objects. This book is invaluable for building more inclusive and equitable classrooms.

Gollub, Matthew. *Ten Oni Drummers.* Illus. Kazuko G. Stone. New York: Lee & Low, 2000. **(M, X)**

A dreaming Japanese boy watches 10 brightly colored, claw-fingered oni emerge one by one from the shore's edge to frolic and make music. The narrator relates that instead of being menacing, oni protect sleeping children from evil; endnotes give more information about these figures from Japanese folklore.

Greenway, Shirley. *Two's Company.* Photos. Oxford Scientific Films. Watertown, MA: Charlesbridge, 1997.

With large, action-filled photographs, this book introduces children to the collective nouns of various animal groups. It

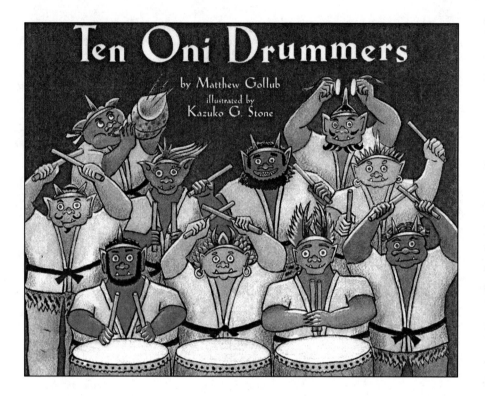

follows the pattern of showing 1 animal, then 2, and then the group, such as a herd of zebras, a train of camels, and a skulk of foxes. Endnotes give additional information that invites further research.

Guy, Ginger Foglesong. *Fiesta!* Illus. René King Moreno. New York: Greenwillow Books, 1996. **(M, X)**

Readers learn to count in both English and Spanish in this bilingual text that depicts children gathering special treats for a party. The predictable text is accessible for beginning readers, and the illustrations show aspects of Mexican culture.

Hamm, Diane Johnston. *How Many Feet in the Bed?* Illus. Kate Salley Palmer. New York: Simon & Schuster, 1991.

Dad is resting in bed early one morning, but as his three children and wife crowd in, the number of feet increases: 2, 4, 6, 8, 10. After a brief, comfy cuddle, the number of feet then decreases by 2s as various events cause each person to leave.

Hendra, Sue. *Numbers.* Cambridge, MA: Candlewick Press, 1999. **(X)**

> This puzzle book follows a predictable format: an animal asks a number-related question on one page; the opposite page contains three flaps concealing possible answers, which are represented by the numeral, the written word, and an array of the corresponding number of dots. Although only one of the possibilities answers the question, the other choices provide interesting facts about animals that will delight emergent readers.

Hoban, Tana. *Let's Count.* New York: Greenwillow Books, 2000.

> Hoban's inviting photographs encourage children to group and count familiar objects (up to 100) in a variety of ways. A particular strength of the book is that each number is represented as a numeral, the number word, a string of white dots (up to 10, then two columns), and a picture.

Hoban, Tana. *More, Fewer, Less.* New York: Greenwillow Books, 1998.

> In her characteristically inviting photographs, Tana Hoban depicts varying quantities of natural and manufactured objects. Discussions about the pictures can make mathematical vocabulary meaningful, especially for young children or second language learners.

Hoberman, Mary Ann. *One of Each.* Illus. Marjorie Priceman. Boston: Little, Brown, 1997.

> Oliver Tolliver lives all alone in his little house, content that he has one of everything. But he soon realizes it is more fun to have two of everything and share them with a friend.

Isadora, Rachel. *1 2 3 Pop!* New York: Viking, 2000.

> The vibrant pop art of this counting book will entice readers to use a variety of counting strategies. Numbers from 1 to 20 and then 100, 500, 1,000, and finally 1,000,000 are represented with pictures, many of which are systematically arranged, such as arrays for square numbers, a triangular formation for 15 (1 + 2 + 3 + 4 + 5), and equal sets for even numbers.

Kaopuiki, Stacey. *Bring Me What I Ask: A Hawaiian Story about Numbers.* Maui, Hawaii: Hawaiian Island Concepts, 1991. **(M, X)**

> A mean troll captures the sun and demands a series of gifts (counting from 1 to 10) before he will restore the light. The

brief text shows counting in English, Hawaiian, and sign languages and depicts objects that are related to Hawaiian culture: the nene and mynah birds, fishhooks of wood and bone, guava jelly, and volcanoes.

Kusugak, Michael Arvaarluk, and Vladyana Krykorka. *My Arctic 1, 2, 3.* Toronto: Annick Press, 1996. **(M, X)**

Readers are introduced to animals of the Arctic in this informative and colorful text. The author explains the relationship between predators and prey and relates his personal experiences with these animals.

Lee, Chinlun. *The Very Kind Rich Lady and Her One Hundred Dogs.* Cambridge, MA: Candlewick Press, 2001.

Every day a very kind rich lady feeds, grooms, and cares for her 100 dogs. Each dog has a special name, and the watercolor illustrations capture each dog's personality.

Lesser, Carolyn. *Spots: Counting Creatures from Sky to Sea.* Illus. Laura Regan. San Diego: Harcourt Brace, 1999. **(X)**

Ten species of variously spotted animals, one from each of Earth's 10 biomes, undulate, leap, or swim across each double-page spread of this multilayered book. The poetic text begs to be read aloud, and informational notes at the end inspire further research.

Luciani, Brigitte. *How Will We Get to the Beach?* Illus. Eve Tharlet. New York: North-South Books, 2000.

Roxanne attempts to travel to the beach with her baby and four objects: a turtle, an umbrella, a thick book, and a ball, but every form of travel (except the last) leaves out one member of the group. Children will love to participate in guessing the outcome of each mode of transportation.

Mannis, Celeste Davidson. *One Leaf Rides the Wind: Counting in a Japanese Garden.* Illus. Susan Kathleen Hartung. New York: Viking, 2002. **(M, X)**

Eleven haiku poems capture the beauty and simplicity of a traditional Japanese garden. Additional brief notes further describe aspects of Japanese culture, and Susan Hartung's rich illustrations extend the peaceful tone of this unusual counting book.

McBratney, Sam. *Guess How Much I Love You.* Illus. Anita Jeram. Cambridge, MA: Candlewick Press, 1995.

> During a bedtime game, Little Nutbrown Hare shows how much he loves his father. With each response, Big Nutbrown Hare demonstrates that he loves his son even more. The story portrays a warm relationship about things that are immeasurable.

McGrath, Barbara Barbieri. *The Baseball Counting Book.* Illus. Brian Shaw. Watertown, MA: Charlesbridge, 1999.

> This counting book uses the numbers 1 to 20 to introduce readers to various aspects of the game of baseball. A full count, for instance, uses 5 fingers; 6 infielders hear the coach's instructions; and spectators stand for the seventh-inning stretch.

Miller, Virginia. *Ten Red Apples: A Bartholomew Bear Counting Book.* Cambridge, MA: Candlewick Press, 2002.

> Bartholomew Bear plays around an apple tree as 10 green apples turn red one by one. The Big Book format clearly shows the part-to-whole relationship. Apples are also counted in a column on the left page, highlighting the odd/even pattern.

Root, Phyllis. *One Duck Stuck.* Illus. Jane Chapman. New York: Scholastic, 1998.

> In this lively, predictable book, a series of animals come to the aid of one duck that is stuck in the mud. The language, illustrations, and format invite readers' active participation; they can chant the repetitive phrases and echoic words *(slosh, slosh; pleep, pleep),* count each group of animals, predict the next group, and dramatize the story.

Stevens, Jan Romero. *Twelve Lizards Leaping: A New Twelve Days of Christmas.* Illus. Christine Mau. Flagstaff, AZ: Rising Moon, 1999.

> Luminaria, coyotes, and prickly pears are among the southwestern sights featured in this adaptation of the traditional Christmas song. The bold acrylic illustrations and lively type invite the reader to count and sing along.

Thorne-Thomsen, Kathleen, and Paul Rocheleau. *A Shaker's Dozen.* San Francisco: Chronicle Books, 1999. **(X)**

> The photographs of Shaker life and artifacts, including tools, rugs, pies, and hats, encourage readers to count using various

strategies (e.g., counting 3 sets of 4 pies), to look for geometric patterns, and to learn about Shaker culture. Endnotes provide additional information and may inspire further research.

Torres, Leyla. *Saturday Sancocho.* New York: Farrar, Straus and Giroux, 1995. **(M)**

Young Maria accompanies her grandmother to the market to purchase ingredients for a delectable stew, chicken *sancocho.* Although the market has only a dozen eggs, grandmother does some shrewd bartering, and they return home with all they need. The illustrations complement the text by illuminating details of Latino culture.

Walton, Rick. *So Many Bunnies: A Bedtime ABC and Counting Book.* Illus. Paige Miglio. New York: Lothrop, Lee & Shepard/ Morrow, 1998.

The names of each of the 26 sleepy bunnies in this rhymed text are sequenced alphabetically. Children can count all 26 and their mother on the last page. The soft watercolor illustrations create a calm, bedtime mood.

Williams, Sue. *Dinnertime!* Illus. Kerry Argent. San Diego: Harcourt, 2001.

A hungry fox is on the prowl, and one by one 6 baby rabbits escape his grasp just in time. The illustrations convey several mathematical patterns, such as the successive subtraction pattern of 6 − 1 = 5, 5 − 1 = 4, as well as different addend combinations for numbers 1 to 6. Best of all, there is a surprise ending that young readers will enjoy.

Winter, Jeanette. *Josefina.* San Diego: Harcourt Brace, 1996. **(M, X)**

This beautiful counting book was inspired by Josefina Aguilar, a beloved Mexican folk artist who lives in Ocotlan and still creates clay figures. The colorful acrylic illustrations show many aspects of Mexican life, such as homes, merchants, farmers, and mariachi music.

Zaslavsky, Claudia. *Count on Your Fingers African Style.* Illus. Wangechi Mutu. New York: Writers and Readers/Black Butterfly Books, 1999.

With colorful and inviting paintings that capture the energy and liveliness of the village marketplace, this book depicts traditional finger counting of various African peoples. It explores the practicality of mathematics within the context of African culture and celebrates the cultural diversity and inventiveness of African peoples.

Number Operations

Aker, Suzanne. *What Comes in 2's, 3's, and 4's?* Illus. Bernie Karlin. New York: Simon & Schuster, 1990.

Bold, bright pictures and a simple question-and-answer format show different contexts for grouping, such as natural sets (poison ivy leaves, dogs' legs), conventional groupings (fork, knife, and spoon), and opposites (up, down). The mathematical potential is rich, including congruence (matching), symmetry, a set model of multiplication, and classification.

Anno, Mitsumasa. *Anno's Magic Seeds.* New York: Philomel, 1995.

Related in a folktale style and illustrated with pleasing watercolors, this book tells the story of Jack and his magic seeds, given to him by a wizard. Each seed bears a plant containing 2 more seeds, and readers witness the doubling power of multiplication.

Appelt, Kathi. *Bat Jamboree.* Illus. Melissa Sweet. New York: Morrow, 1996.

Readers count sets of bats from 1 to 10 as they fly into a meadow to join the jamboree. Finally, these 10 sets of bats are shown in a pyramid formation, highlighting the triangular number of 55. Children might investigate making other triangular numbers.

Appelt, Kathi. *Bats on Parade*. Illus. Melissa Sweet. New York: Mulberry, 1998.

Lively rhyme and comical illustrations invite readers to join the crowd that watches the bats' grand marching band. The instrumental groups march in perfect arrays of consecutive square numbers, culminating with 100 sousaphones in 10 rows of 10, nicely demonstrating an area model of multiplication.

Birch, David. *The King's Chessboard.* Illus. Devis Grebu. New York: Dial, 1988.

A king wants to reward his grand counselor for all his helpfulness over the years. In lieu of gold, jewels, and palaces, the counselor chooses the humble gift of rice: grains of rice doubled each day for 32 days. When the granaries of the kingdom are depleted, the king seeks a reprieve from the request, and he learns a lesson about humility at the same time.

Bourke, Linda. *Eye Count: A Book of Counting Puzzles.* San Francisco: Chronicle Books, 1995. **(X)**

Here is an intriguing riddle counting book in which readers must figure out the connection between the various objects on the page. The pictures contain objects that are either homophones—such as a musical *chord* and a *cord* of wood—or homonyms—such as the *jack* in a deck of cards and a phone *jack.*

Clement, Rod. *Counting on Frank.* Milwaukee, WI: Gareth Stevens, 1991.

Accompanied by his dog Frank, a young boy uses objects in his house as the basis for some amusing calculations. He calculates, for instance, the number of dogs he could fit in his bedroom and how long it would take to fill the bathroom with water. The book can inspire children to perform some of their own calculations.

Cuyler, Margery. *100th Day Worries.* Illus. Arthur Howard. New York: Simon & Schuster, 2000.

Children will identify with Jessica, who can't find a satisfactory collection of 100 items for the school celebration despite her family's willingness to help. Cartoon illustrations portray Jessica's emotions, her clever solution, and a variety of groupings that make up 100, such as 5 bags of 20 peanuts, 10 piles of 10 paper clips, and 4 jars of 25 peppermints.

Dee, Ruby, reteller. *Two Ways to Count to Ten: A Liberian Folktale.* Illus. Susan Meddaugh. New York: Henry Holt, 1988. **(M)**

In order to find a suitable successor, a leopard king challenges his subjects to throw a spear high enough to be able to count to 10 before it reaches the ground. Antelope's solution, to count by 2s, makes this Liberian tale a good introduction to multiplication by repeated addition.

Demi. *One Grain of Rice.* New York: Scholastic, 1997. **(M)**

In this traditional Indian tale, farmers face starvation until Rani tricks the greedy raja into rewarding her for a good deed by giving her a grain of rice, doubled each day for 30 days.

Foldout pages convey the growth rate of this geometric progression.

Dodds, Dayle Ann. *The Great Divide.* Illus. Tracy Mitchell. Cambridge, MA: Candlewick Press, 1999.

In this fanciful rhymed story, a group of bicycle racers diminishes page by page as the riders encounter a series of obstacles and disasters. The original number of 80 is successively halved in an 80 – 40 – 20 – 10 – 5 pattern; the pattern is cleverly modified to designate a single winner.

Enzensberger, Hans Magnus. *The Number Devil: A Mathematical Adventure.* Illus. Rotraut Susanne Berner. Trans. Michael Henry Heim. New York: Henry Holt, 2000.

Dismayed by the math instruction he receives in school, twelve-year-old Robert discovers in his dreams the fascinating world of numbers when he meets a number devil. With a wry sense of humor, the devil introduces such topics as infinity, odd and even numbers, factors, Fibonacci sequence, permutations, and more.

Friedman, Aileen. *The King's Commissioners.* Illus. Susan Guevara. New York: Scholastic, 1994.

A worried king fears he has been appointing too many royal counselors and decides to count them. One advisor counts by 2s and tallies 23 with a remainder of 1. Another counts by 5s and tallies nine 5s with a remainder of 2. The king is infuriated with the apparent discrepancy, but his daughter assures him the amounts are equivalent by teaching him about place value.

Giganti, Paul Jr. *Each Orange Had 8 Slices: A Counting Book.* Illus. Donald Crews. New York: Greenwillow Books, 1992.

Questions on each page ask readers to count sets of objects shown in the illustrations, such as 2 cows, each with 2 calves that, in turn, have 4 skinny legs. The book invites readers to count-on, using a set model for multiplication, as well as to use Giganti's pattern for their own writing.

Ginsburg, Mirra, adapter. *Two Greedy Bears.* Illus. Jose Aruego and Ariane Dewey. New York: Aladdin, 1998.

This Hungarian folktale relates the story of two bears that cannot agree on a way to divide a round cheese into two equal portions. A sly fox seizes the opportunity to consume most of the cheese, and the bears are left with two equal but tiny shares.

Gorbachev, Valeri. *Nicky and the Big, Bad Wolves.* New York: North-South Books, 1998.

A baby rabbit named Nicky wakes up from a bad dream, imagining that 100 wolves are chasing him. When questioned by his mother, he revises his estimate to 50 wolves, then 15, and finally 5. Mother finally chases all the bad wolves by banging on some garbage cans. This book provides a good context for discussing the strategy of estimation.

Guettier, Bénédicte. *The Father Who Had 10 Children.* New York: Dial, 1999.

In this humorous story, a father decides to take a break from his 10 very busy children, only to find that the opposite of very busy is lonely! Both the story and the large illustrations invite skip counting by 1s, 2s, 5s, and 10s as the father prepares different kinds of food for 10 (e.g., bowls of cereal, piles of raspberries) in various quantities.

Harris, Trudy. *100 Days of School.* Illus. Beth Griffis Johnson. Brookfield, CT: Millbrook Press, 1999.

Much more than an exploration of the 100th day, this book uses a range of combinations and contexts for this special number. Many of the examples use benchmark numbers such as 10, 25, or 50 and demonstrate both addition and multiplication. The humorous tone, riddles, and jokes add to the appeal.

Harshman, Marc. *Only One.* Illus. Barbara Garrison. New York: Cobblehill Books/Dutton, 1993.

Centered on a country fair, this text features sets of things in the world. It shows large numbers, such as one million stars and 50,000 honeybees, as well as smaller numbers, such as a dozen eggs, 4 wheels on a cart, and 3 musicians. The illustrations, made from a collage/printing process, give a warm, homey feel to the country setting.

Hoban, Tana. *26 Letters and 99 Cents.* New York: Greenwillow Books, 1987.

An alphabet and a counting book are combined in this colorful, eye-appealing text of photographs. Puffy, bright letters of the alphabet make up one-half of the book, and actual-size pictures of coins introduce children to pennies, nickels, dimes, and quarters in the other half. The use of coins for counting can prompt children to think of other possible coin combinations for each value shown.

Hong, Lily Toy, reteller. *Two of Everything: A Chinese Folktale.* Morton Grove, IL: Albert Whitman, 1992. **(M)**

In this amusing Chinese folktale, a farmer discovers a magic pot that doubles the quantity of anything put inside it. He and his wife happily envision their fortunes until first one and then the other falls into the pot.

Hulme, Joy N. *Sea Squares.* Illus. Carol Schwartz. New York: Hyperion, 1991. **(X)**

Each page of this rhymed text uses a number from 1 to 10 in two ways: the members of a set (e.g., 3 clown fish) and an equal number of one of their attributes (3 stripes), calculated as a total square number (9). Lovely illustrations and information in the endnotes can inspire further research.

Hutchins, Pat. *The Doorbell Rang.* New York: Greenwillow Books, 1986.

An appealing choice for many years, this book inspires a range of mathematical and literary responses. A steady stream of children arrives at the door, making it necessary to recalculate equal shares of Grandma's 12 cookies, but Grandma herself saves the day.

Johnson, Angela. *One of Three.* Illus. David Soman. New York: Orchard, 1995. **(M)**

The narrator of this story loves being included in outings with her two older sisters, but when she's not included, she finds comfort in being "one of three" with her parents instead. The book invites children to tell their own family stories and to describe subsets of their family according to interests or activities.

MacDonald, Suse. *Look Whooo's Counting.* New York: Scholastic, 2000.

On the simplest level, this predictable book counts from 1 to 10, but the bold cut-paper illustrations invite further explorations with patterns of square numbers. The sets of animals that Owl counts hide numerals in their bodies, such as 6 in the six sheep's horns, while Owl's outstretched wings frame the appropriate counting sequence (1, 2, 3, 4, 5, 6).

Mathews, Louise. *Gator Pie.* Illus. Jeni Bassett. Littleton, MA: Sundance, 1995.

Two alligators' plan to share a large pie goes awry when more and more demanding gators come upon the scene, but quick thinking saves the day. Thought bubbles illustrate the quickly changing size of slices; these diagrams as well as the story create a rich potential for discussing an area model of fractions.

Merriam, Eve. *12 Ways to Get to 11.* Illus. Barnie Karlin. New York: Simon & Schuster, 1993.

Many of these twelve ways to "get to 11" include three or more addends, making this book a valuable choice when exploring equivalence. Various examples can also lead to other topics, such as odd and even numbers or a set model of multiplication.

Moss, Lloyd. *Zin! Zin! Zin! A Violin.* Illus. Marjorie Priceman. Simon & Schuster, 1995. **(X)**

As a chamber orchestra (10 instruments total) assembles, the growing group is identified by its number: solo, duet, trio, quartet, quintet, sextet, septet, octet, nonet. Elongated, supple figures, vibrant colors, and rhythmic verses arranged in curved lines all work together to make this book a musical feast.

Napoli, Donna Jo, and Richard Tchen. *How Hungry Are You?* Illus. Amy Walrod. New York: Atheneum, 2001.

Two friends plan a picnic together, but sets of other picnickers keep joining the group, and there is much discussion about how to divide the food. The story makes extensive use of dialogue, which children might enjoy exploring through readers' theater.

Pallotta, Jerry. *The Icky Bug Counting Book.* Illus. Ralph Mansiello. Watertown, MA: Charlesbridge, 1992.

Only after reading this text do children realize that this counting book is also an alphabet book! Interesting facts about beetles, weevils, spiders, wasps, ants, glowworms, and more fill each page.

Pérez, L. King. *First Day in Grapes.* Illus. Robert Casilla. New York: Lee & Low, 2002. **(M)**

Chico earns respect for the mental computational ability he has developed while counting crates of produce picked by his papá, a migrant farmer. This simple story teaches valuable lessons about tolerance, conflict resolution, and belief in oneself.

Pinczes, Elinor J. *A Remainder of One.* Illus. Bonnie MacKain. Boston: Houghton Mifflin, 1995.

Joe, one of 25 ants, is constantly a remainder when his troop of ants marches in rows of 2, 3, and 4. He finally fits in when they march in 5 rows of 5. Children are particularly drawn to the plight of Joe. Another, related book about marching ants is *One Hundred Hungry Ants* (1993).

Pittman, Helena Clare. *A Grain of Rice.* New York: Bantam Skylark, 1986. **(M)**

When a humble farmer is denied the hand of the emperor's daughter in marriage, he devises a clever mathematical plan to change the decision. This Chinese variant of the well-known Indian tale shows the explosive power of a geometric progression.

Pomeroy, Diana. *One Potato: A Counting Book of Potato Prints.* San Diego: Harcourt Brace, 1996.

Soft, rounded fruits and vegetables spill over the frames on each page of this beautiful counting book (1 to 10, 20, 40, 50, 100). Children can discuss strategies for mental addition suggested by the clusters and groupings of objects. Instructions for potato printing are included.

Ross, Tony. *Centipede's 100 Shoes.* New York: Henry Holt, 2002.

A centipede with sore feet buys shoes and socks but finds them too bothersome to put on and so gives them away to creatures with fewer legs (a good math problem to solve). The watercolor illustrations enhance the humor of this silly tale.

Ryan, Pam Muñoz. *One Hundred Is a Family.* Illus. Benrei Huang. New York: Hyperion, 1994. **(M)**

In this thematic counting book, the author depicts different kinds of families as she counts from 1 to 10 and then by 10s to 100. The people in the text are connected by family, friendship, and community, thus providing readers with an invitation to talk about traditional and nontraditional families.

Sayre, April Pulley, and Jeff Sayre. *One Is a Snail, Ten Is a Crab.* Illus. Randy Cecil. Cambridge, MA: Candlewick Press, 2003.

> Creatures with different numbers of feet march off to the beach and provide interesting contexts for counting (1 to 10 and by 10s to 100). For instance, 60 legs are shown as 6 crabs (10 legs each) or 10 insects (6 legs each). Large, clear illustrations make the sets easy to count.

Schwartz, David M. *How Much Is a Million?* Illus. Steven Kellogg. New York: Lothrop, Lee & Shepard, 1985.

> The relative magnitudes of million, billion, and trillion are conveyed through a series of intriguing comparisons. Steven Kellogg's fun-filled, humorous illustrations enhance the lighthearted tone of the book. Helpful endnotes inform readers about how the author did his calculating.

Schwartz, David M. *On beyond a Million: An Amazing Math Journey.* Illus. Paul Meisel. New York: Random House, 1999.

> Professor X and his dog Y lead a group of children in exploring the meanings of very large numbers. This complex topic is made accessible through a clever format that includes answers to children's questions shown in speech bubbles (and based on the author's experience working with students) and sidebars that apply large quantities to the real world.

Scieszka, Jon. *Math Curse.* Illus. Lane Smith. New York: Viking, 1995.

> Illustrations + story line + typeface + wordplay = an unforgettable mathematical and literary spoof in which a "math-cursed" girl sees everything around her as a math problem. Every detail of the book, including the date of publication and the author/illustrator biographical notes, fits the theme.

Sturges, Philemon. *Ten Flashing Fireflies.* Illus. Anna Vojtech. New York: North-South Books, 1995.

> The soft glow of fireflies against a dark sky conveys the wonder and delight of capturing these insects on a summer's night. The illustrations show the full set of 10 fireflies, some in and some out of the jar, until all are released at the book's end.

Tang, Greg. *The Grapes of Math: Mind-Stretching Math Riddles.* Illus. Harry Briggs. New York: Scholastic, 2001.

> Each illustrated riddle invites children to look for visual patterns and groupings of objects in order to calculate sums

strategically and efficiently. Teachers might share this book by showing the pictures first, allowing children to discuss possible strategies, and then reading Tang's suggested solution. See also *Math for All Seasons* (2002) and *Math Appeal* (2003).

Trivas, Irene. *Emma's Christmas: An Old Song.* New York: Orchard Books, 1988.

This version of the familiar song "The Twelve Days of Christmas" has a special twist: Emma, the farmer's daughter, is not impressed with the increasing numbers of gifts sent by a love-stricken prince. The book can encourage explorations in mathematics (calculating the total number of gifts and exploring number patterns) and in literature (character analysis, dramatization, and studies of folktales).

Wahl, John, and Stacey Wahl. *I Can Count the Petals of a Flower.* Reston, VA: National Council of Teachers of Mathematics, 1976. **(X)**

The authors spent twenty years traveling around the globe to photograph flowers that were composed of varying numbers of petals. The exquisite results are arranged in two sections: the first features one labeled flower on each page, whereas the second uses individual flowers for prime numbers and sets of flowers for composite numbers.

Walton, Rick. *How Many, How Many, How Many.* Illus. Cynthia Jabar. Cambridge, MA: Candlewick Press, 1993.

This book explores the many contexts of sets in the everyday world, such as 4 seasons, 5 fingers, 7 colors in the rainbow, 9 planets, and 12 months. Children will enjoy counting the objects in the pictures and finding more examples of sets for their own collections.

Wells, Rosemary. *Emily's First 100 Days of School.* New York: Hyperion, 2000.

Children in Emily's class cumulatively represent the first 100 days of school using a variety of contexts and associations. Most of the examples illustrate various uses for numbers, such as monetary value (25 cents in a quarter), linear measurement (36 inches in a yard), and organizational tools (street numbers), thus inspiring readers to search for numbers in their own lives.

Wheeler, Lisa. *Sixteen Cows.* Illus. Kurt Cyrus. San Diego: Harcourt, 2002.

This is a rhyming tale of Cowboy Gene and Cowgirl Sue whose cows (8 each) get mixed up when a storm blows down the fence between the two herds. It's a humorous scene when each tries to sing the herd to his or her side of the pasture. Marriage brings Gene and Sue together, along with their two herds.

Informational Resource Books

Ash, Russell. *Incredible Comparisons.* New York: DK, 1996. **(X)**

Understanding the magnitude of large numbers can be a difficult task. The author addresses this problem by creating a wide range of comparisons related to the universe, weather, animal speed, mountains, the solar system, big buildings, and others. The illustrations enhance understanding through large-scale comparison and familiar objects for comparing, such as the human body, the Empire State Building, or bathtubs of liquid.

Ash, Russell. *The Top Ten of Everything 2002.* New York: DK, 2002. **(X)**

Lists of the top ten of almost everything imaginable crowd this volume: musicians, movies, sporting events, libraries, planets, animal life, etc. In a large format and replete with photographs, this text will be referred to again and again by upper elementary children.

Ash, Russell. *The World in One Day.* New York: DK, 1997. **(X)**

What happens in one day in the life of the world? So begins a fascinating look at such happenings as they relate to animals, the human body, waste and recycling, plants, communication, travel, and others. Interesting visual displays of the data make this text an appealing read.

Gates, Phil. *Nature Got There First: Inventions Inspired by Nature.* New York: Kingfisher, 1995. **(X)**

Through accessible and engaging narratives, diagrams, and photographs, this book illustrates parallel principles of engineering in nature and the manufactured world. Topics include structural design, strength of materials, mechanisms for defense and protection, motion and movement, tools, sensory aids, energy, and chemistry.

Hertzberg, Hendrik. *One Million.* New York: Times Books, 1993. **(X)**

> Each page of this book contains a triangular shape of dots, and when added together, they total one million. To help readers better understand the relative magnitude of large numbers, the author has provided statistics related to such topics as population, religion, transportation, etc.

Lankford, Mary D. *Dominoes around the World.* Illus. Karen Dugan. New York: Morrow, 1998. **(M, X)**

> In a colorful, easy-to-read format, the author traces the history of dominoes and explains the different variations of the game in eight countries. Helpful background information about each country and illustrations enhance the multicultural context of this resource. See also *Jacks around the World* (1996).

Maganzini, Christy. *Cool Math.* Illus. Ruta Daugavietis. Los Angeles: Price Stern Sloan, 1997. **(M)**

> In a humorous and conversational style, the author introduces readers to a variety of math tricks, puzzles, and real-world applications to computers and the natural world. Included are numerous patterns for exploring and interesting facts from the history of mathematics.

Morgan, Rowland. *In the Next Three Seconds.* Illus. Rod Josey and Kira Josey. New York: Puffin, 1999. **(X)**

> Using a variety of statistics related to transportation, food consumption, ecological issues, and others, the author predicts what will happen in the near and distant future. He uses intervals of 3 seconds, 3 hours, 3 days, 3 years, 3 decades, 3 centuries, 3,000 years, and 3 million years. Children can use the information to make some of their own predictions.

Pike, Robert W. *Checker Power: A Game of Problem Solving.* Watertown, MA: Charlesbridge, 1997.

> The author begins with a brief history of the game of checkers and the current rules. He then describes nine key strategies for becoming a skillful player, such as controlling the middle of the board and protecting the back row. The illustrations are clear and easy to follow.

Rice, David L. *Lifetimes.* Illus. Michael S. Maydak. Nevada City, CA: Dawn, 1997. **(X)**

Species of plants and animals are arranged in order of longevity, from the mayfly (one day) to a sequoia (2,000 years), followed by related facts about the Earth and solar system. Each page also includes suggested activities that allow readers to explore the various statistics.

Ross, Kathy. *Kathy Ross Crafts Numbers.* Illus. Jan Barger. Brookfield, CT: Millbrook Press, 2003.

This activity book demonstrates how simple crafts made from everyday materials can help children learn the shapes of numerals, the values of each number, and the purposes of measuring tools. See also *Kathy Ross Crafts Triangles, Rectangles, Circles, and Squares* (2002) for activities that address concepts in geometry.

Schmandt-Besserat, Denise. *The History of Counting.* Illus. Michael Hays. New York: Morrow, 1999. **(M, X)**

Eminent archaeologist Denise Schmandt-Besserat provides a historical and cultural perspective on the wide range of purposes for and forms of representation among the world's numeration systems. Through this book, readers will better understand and appreciate that mathematical systems are invented and that their levels of abstraction and precision reflect the purposes they serve, rather than the intelligence of the inventors.

Schwartz, David M. *G Is for Googol: A Math Alphabet Book.* Illus. Marissa Moss. Berkeley, CA: Tricycle Press, 1998. **(M, X)**

From *A* to *Z,* readers learn about the history and significance of such ideas as cubits, tessellations, light years, and exponents. The author's trademark wit and the colorful illustrations make this an appealing resource for children.

Seabrooke, Kevin, ed. *The World Almanac for Kids 2003.* Mahwah, NJ: World Almanac Books, 2002.

Here is a compendium of intriguing facts and figures—e.g., top-selling toys, inventions, overview of environmental problems, data on all the nations of the world, and statistics about the human body. Maps, time lines, photographs, and charts make this a visually interesting text.

Sullivan, George. *Any Number Can Play: The Numbers Athletes Wear.* Illus. Anne Canevari Green. Brookfield, CT: Millbrook Press, 2000. **(X)**

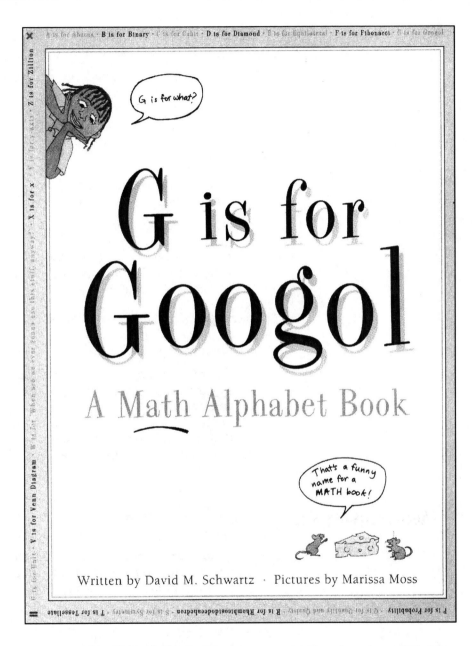

This book is packed with amusing cartoon drawings and short anecdotes about number-related sports trivia. It explains how jersey numbers were designed to correspond to field positions in several sports, and reveals humorous, historical, and touching details about many famous sports figures.

Wyatt, Valerie. *The Math Book for Girls and Other Beings Who Count.* Illus. Pat Cupples. Toronto: Kids Can Press, 2000. **(X)**

This book is replete with engaging mathematical puzzles and activities, and serves a second important purpose: to specifically connect the content of these activities to careers in mathematics and science. Set-off boxes describe female biologists, financial advisors, and other professionals engaged in their work.

Zaslavsky, Claudia. *More Math Games & Activities from around the World.* Chicago: Chicago Review Press, 2003. **(M, X)**

Over 70 games and projects stretch children's mathematical reasoning, strategies, and skills while providing windows into cultures from around the globe. These activities range from simple to challenging. See also *Math Games & Activities from around the World* (1998).

Zaslavsky, Claudia. *Number Sense and Nonsense: Building Math Creativity and Confidence through Number Play.* Chicago: Chicago Review Press, 2001. **(M, X)**

The format and design of this book will engage readers in explorations across many mathematical topics, including odd and even numbers, prime and composite numbers, measurement, riddles, numeration systems, and calculator tricks. Biographical, historical, and cross-cultural information make the book valuable as a more general resource as well.

Measurement

Adler, David A. *America's Champion Swimmer: Gertrude Ederle.* Illus. Terry Widener. San Diego: Harcourt, 2000. **(X)**

In addition to being an Olympic champion, Gertrude Ederle became the first woman to swim the English Channel. Mathematical details about time, distance, and the size of the waves contribute to her inspiring story.

Anno, Mitsumasa. *All in a Day.* Illus. Raymond Briggs et al. New York: Philomel, 1986. **(M)**

Double-page spreads introduce readers to the concept of time zones as the text follows the lives of nine children in different locations throughout the world. The illustrations of a variety of multicultural artists are featured in this story. An excellent afterword includes a map and explains how time zones work.

Brisson, Pat. *Benny's Pennies.* Illus. Bob Barner. New York: Doubleday, 1993.

> Benny clutches 5 new pennies as he goes off to buy treats for his family. A predictable text with lovely collage illustrations, this story shows Benny spending one penny at a time for a rose, a cookie, a paper hat, and other special surprises.

Brown, Don. *Alice Ramsey's Grand Adventure.* Boston: Houghton Mifflin, 1997.

> In 1909, Alice Ramsey became the first woman to drive a car from coast to coast. She and her three passengers (none of whom drove) faced mechanical difficulties, floods, and bad weather, but after 59 courageous days, they completed their journey.

Chinn, Karen. *Sam and the Lucky Money.* Illus. Cornelius Van Wright and Ying-Hwa Hu. New York: Lee & Low, 1995. **(M)**

> It is New Year's Day, and Sam has just received some money from his grandparents. He sets off for Chinatown to do some shopping but finally decides to spend the money on a person in need. Warm watercolor paintings capture the sights and sounds of Chinese American culture.

Facklam, Margery. *The Big Bug Book.* Illus. Paul Facklam. Boston: Little, Brown, 1994.

> The author introduces readers to thirteen of the world's largest insects, such as the praying mantis, the walking stick, and the Madagascar hissing cockroach. Children get a real sense of the size of these creatures because the illustrations are life-size, and they show bugs against a familiar context (such as the goliath beetle on a plate of cookies).

Harper, Dan. *Telling Time with Big Mama Cat.* Illus. Barry Moser and Cara Moser. San Diego: Harcourt Brace, 1998.

> Featuring a clock with movable hands, this story describes a cat and her daily activities. Increments of one hour predominate, but 5, 15, and 30 minutes are also shown. A sense of humor is wonderfully displayed throughout as the cat scratches a couch, licks some dirty dishes, and eats out of the dog's dish.

Inkpen, Mick. *The Great Pet Sale.* New York: Orchard Books, 1999.

> A young boy is attracted by a sale at a pet store and must

decide what to buy. After surveying the prices of many creatures, he realizes that his $1.00 will enable him to buy them all. The grouping of some creatures, such as the salamander, skink, and gecko, may invite further research on their differences.

Jenkins, Steve. *Big & Little.* Boston: Houghton Mifflin, 1996.

Using crisp cut-paper collages, the author introduces readers to a wide range of different-size animals found throughout the world. A scale drawing allows readers to compare these animals, and endnotes give additional information on each creature.

Jenkins, Steve. *Biggest, Strongest, Fastest.* New York: Tichnor & Fields, 1995.

Readers learn about the world record holders in the animal kingdom: the biggest and smallest, the fastest and slowest, and the strongest and longest. A silhouette comparison on each page relates these animal abilities and measurements to those of a human.

Jenkins, Steve. *Hottest, Coldest, Highest, Deepest.* Boston: Houghton Mifflin, 1998. **(X)**

Geographical data are brought to life in this visually appealing text. Statistics are made relevant through the use of global and regional maps, diagrams, and charts that use humans and the Empire State Building as a scale for better understanding. Text and illustrations work together to make a clear and intriguing format.

Lasky, Kathryn. *The Man Who Made Time Travel.* Illus. Kevin Hawkes. New York: Melanie Kroups Books, 2003. **(X)**

This engaging biography relates how John Harrison developed a timepiece that could operate successfully even on rough seas, thus enabling navigators to accurately measure longitude. Lasky chronicles Harrison's problem-solving strategies as well as his inspirational persistence, two important attitudes in today's mathematics classrooms.

Lasky, Kathryn. *The Most Beautiful Roof in the World: Exploring the Rainforest Canopy.* Photos. Christopher G. Knight. San Diego: Harcourt Brace, 1997. **(X)**

Meg Lowman traces her interest in botany from her elementary school years, when she won her state's science fair competition, to her current research of the rain forest canopy. The book demonstrates real-life applications of data collection and measurement, as well as the role of women in scientific careers.

Lee, Spike, and Tonya Lewis Lee. *Please, Baby, Please.* Simon & Schuster, 2002. **(M)**

Despite parental pleas, Baby bounds through a day filled with typical toddler antics. Small clock faces on each page, tracing the time from 3 a.m. to 10 p.m., add a layer of information that increases the humor of the text and illustrations.

Maestro, Betsy. *The Story of Clocks and Calendars: Marking a Millennium.* Illus. Giulio Maestro. New York: Lothrop, Lee & Shepard, 1999. **(M, X)**

This valuable informational book describes how the measurement of time developed from human need and how it has varied across cultures and throughout history. Although the Christian Gregorian calendar is emphasized because of its widespread use, the author also describes the Hebrew, Chinese, and Islamic calendars. She also mentions the current debate about ways to make the Gregorian calendar more inclusive.

McMillan, Bruce. *Jelly Beans for Sale.* New York: Scholastic, 1996.

Children arrive at the jelly bean stand with pennies, dimes, nickels, and quarters; select their favorite colors; and make their purchases. Photographs show the coin combinations clearly. The text includes conventional notation, and endnotes give information on the history and production of jelly beans.

Mollel, Tololwa M. *My Rows and Piles of Coins.* Illus. E. B. Lewis. New York: Clarion Books, 1999. **(M, X)**

In this beautifully illustrated book, Saruni, a young Tanzanian boy, yearns for a new bicycle so that he can better help transport the family produce to the marketplace. When his hard work does not yield the large sum necessary for his purchase, his family helps solve the problem.

Nagda, Ann Whitehead, and Cindy Bickel. *Chimp Math: Learning about Time from a Baby Chimpanzee.* New York: Henry Holt, 2002. **(X)**

Jiggs, a very weak baby chimpanzee, was sent to the Denver Zoo for special care. Photos document his progress in cognitive and motor abilities, while accompanying time lines, charts, and calendars give additional information.

Nagda, Ann Whitehead, and Cindy Bickel. *Tiger Math: Learning to Graph from a Baby Tiger.* New York: Henry Holt, 2000. **(X)**

Two texts—a photographic documentary and an accompanying series of graphs—tell the engaging story of a motherless

Siberian tiger cub's struggle to thrive. A particular strength of the book is that it demonstrates the functional uses of various graphic displays, such as a line graph to trace T. J.'s weight gain and to compare it to his father's record of growth.

Nolan, Helen. *How Much, How Many, How Far, How Heavy, How Long, How Tall Is 1000?* Illus. Tracy Walker. Toronto: Kids Can Press, 1995.

Depending on its context, 1,000 can be a small number (you have many more than 1,000 hairs on your head) or a very large one (you couldn't carry 1,000 pennies even if you used all your pockets). These examples and many others provide accessible benchmarks for 1,000 in such contexts as area, time, distance, and volume.

Parker, Nancy Winslow. *Money, Money, Money: The Meaning of the Art and Symbols on United States Paper Currency.* New York: HarperCollins, 1995. **(X)**

This text describes the fascinating history of paper money in the United States. Topics include the history of the Great Seal, interesting facts about the persons depicted on the bills (mostly presidents, but not all), methods for thwarting counterfeiters, and an overview of the Federal Reserve.

Pollock, Yevonne. *The Old Man's Mitten: A Traditional Tale.* Illus. Trish Hill. Glen Head, NY: Mondo, 1994.

An old man's lost mitten soon becomes a warm home for a mouse, a rabbit, a frog, a fox, a rabbit, and a bear. Humorous illustrations portray the cramped quarters of all the inhabitants!

Schwartz, David M. *If You Hopped Like a Frog.* Illus. James Warhola. New York: Scholastic, 1999. **(X)**

This book piques the mathematical imagination by applying statistics about animals to the human world. Endnotes give further scientific and mathematical information, and the bold cartoon illustrations add humor and delight.

Schwartz, David M. *Millions to Measure.* Illus. Steven Kellogg. New York: HarperCollins, 2003. **(X)**

With his characteristic wit, the author introduces readers to the problems of nonstandard units of measure and then discusses the awkward "customary system" of feet, pounds, and ounces, as well as the more convenient metric system. Steven Kellogg's whimsical illustrations add clarity and humor to this historical account of measurement.

Singer, Marilyn. *Nine o'Clock Lullaby.* Illus. Frané Lessac. New York: HarperCollins, 1991. **(M)**

As they read about a variety of families engaged in daily activities around the world, readers are introduced to the concept of time zones. Specific cultural activities are included, such as the Puerto Rican festival in which musicians play congas and guitars and people eat sweet rice and coconut candy.

Thayer, Tanya. *Spending Money.* Minneapolis: Lerner, 2002.

Through a series of bright color photographs, the author introduces K–1 readers to the many ways that children can spend money. The predictable text shows children buying a variety of items and gives reasons for their actions, such as going somewhere special (the zoo) and helping others (gift giving).

Wells, Robert E. *How Do You Know What Time It Is?* Morton Grove, IL: Albert Whitman, 2002. **(X)**

The author gives a brief history of measuring time: days (shadow, water, and atomic clocks); months (moon cycle); and years (solar calendar). Illustrations are clear and uncluttered, providing additional information to help readers understand this abstract concept.

Wells, Robert E. *Is a Blue Whale the Biggest Thing There Is?* Morton Grove, IL: Albert Whitman, 1993. **(X)**

Here Wells explores the relative size of objects, ranging from an elephant to celestial bodies. Invitations to imagine "bags" of Earths as marbles to compare to the sun, for example, provide some general comparisons and can inspire further research.

Wells, Robert E. *What's Faster Than a Speeding Cheetah?* Morton Grove, IL: Albert Whitman, 1997. **(X)**

A cheetah racing along at 70 mph seems surprisingly slow when compared to jets, meteorites, and the speed of sound and light. In addition to the text and illustrations, a chart comparing the time it would take each to reach the moon makes these rates of speed meaningful for young readers.

Geometry

Agee, Jon. *Sit on a Potato Pan, Otis!* New York: Farrar, Straus and Giroux, 1999.

Agee is the recognized master of word palindromes (words or groups of words that can be read the same way forward and backward). The title of this book is one such example. The letters in "sit on a potato pan, Otis" make the same words from right to left (allowing for different spacing). These word palindromes can be an invitation for children to find numeric ones (55; 121; 4884). By continuing to reverse and add the digits of non-palindromic numbers, one can create palindromes, such as 34 + 43 = 77. Other books in this series include *John Agee's Palindromania* (2002); *Go Hang a Salami! I'm a Lasagna Hog!* (1991); *So Many Dynamos* (1997).

Alda, Arlene. *Arlene Alda's 1 2 3: What Do You See?* Berkeley, CA: Tricycle Press, 1998.

After viewing Alda's captivating photographs, young and old alike will notice the shapes of numerals in natural and manufactured objects. A kite string framed in the sky forms a 2, the handle of a pair of scissors makes a 6, and a fish's gills and eye become a 10. Read also the companion text *Arlene Alda's ABC: What Do You See?* (1993).

Baranski, Joan Sullivan. *Round Is a Pancake.* Illus. Yu-Mei Han. New York: Dutton, 2001.

In this predictable, brief rhyme, readers view some jolly townspeople preparing a delectable feast for their medieval king. Two- and three-dimensional round objects are named on each page, but the illustrations inspire children to find even more.

Birmingham, Duncan. *'M' Is for Mirror.* Norfolk, England: Tarquin, 1988.

To solve each of these challenging puzzles, readers must first use the text clue to infer which object is hidden in the illustration. Next they need to experiment by placing a mirror (provided) on the picture, rotating it, and moving it until the specified object appears.

Burns, Marilyn. *The Greedy Triangle.* Illus. Gordon Silveria. New York: Scholastic, 1994.

A seemingly happy triangle thinks life would be even better if he had just one more side. He goes to the local shapeshifter and has himself transformed into other polygons, only to conclude that life as a triangle is really the best life of all. The story highlights the functional use of shapes as well as the message of being content with one's own abilities.

Cohen, Caron Lee. *Where's the Fly?* Illus. Nancy Barnet. New York: Greenwillow Books, 1996.

Spatial relations are shown through a series of increasingly distant perspectives, from a fly on a dog's nose to a house, a yard, a street corner, and eventually the planet Earth. A series of small pictures at the top of each page serve as placeholders for each successive location.

Crawford, Chris. *Tangram Puzzles: 500 Tricky Shapes to Confound & Astound.* New York: Sterling, 2002.

The author briefly introduces different types of tangram puzzles: standard, paradox, and convex. Five hundred interesting puzzles are classified into birds, buildings, large animals, people, sea life, shoes, tools, transportation, and others.

Elffers, Joost, and Michael Schuyt. *Tangram: The Ancient Chinese Puzzle.* New York: Stewart, Tabori, & Chang, 1997.

Here is the most comprehensive collection of puzzles (1,600 in all) to solve with a set of tangrams. It also includes a brief history of the puzzle and some helpful hints on solving these silhouette pictures.

Feldman, Judy. *Shapes in Nature.* Chicago: Children's Press, 1991. **(X)**

The author uses photographs of scenes in nature and matching black outlines to highlight a variety of shapes such as ovals, circles, triangles, and squares. One of the strengths of this book is that it represents a single shape in different ways, such as a triangle shown as a mountaintop, a fish's fin, the teeth of a shark, and a melting piece of ice.

Fleischman, Paul. *Lost! A Story in String.* Illus. C. B. Mordan. New York: Holt, 2000. **(X)**

While Grandmother tells her young granddaughter a story from her own childhood, she creates a series of string figures to accompany her tale: a gate, a dog's head, the North Star, and five others. Instructions for making Grandmother's figures are included.

Franco, Betsy. *Grandpa's Quilt.* Illus. Linda A. Bild. New York: Children's Press, 1999. **(M)**

Grandpa's loving grandchildren try various ways to cut and resew Grandpa's quilt so that it covers his feet. This easy-to-read text conveys family love and invites further explorations with quilt patterns (squares and triangles) and with an area model of multiplication.

Friedman, Aileen. *A Cloak for the Dreamer.* Illus. Kim Howard. New York: Scholastic, 1994.

In this story, tessellations come into play as a tailor and his three sons make warm cloaks for the archduke. One of the sons, who would rather travel and see the world, mistakenly makes a cloak out of circles, which has many gaps in it. But when the circles are cut and trimmed into hexagons, the pieces fit together. This new cloak is given to the third son as a gift so he can stay warm as he sets out to see the world.

Harris, Trudy. *Pattern Fish.* Illus. Anne Canevari Green. Brookfield, CT: Millbrook Press, 2000. **(X)**

On each page, the color scheme of a sea creature, the single line of text that describes its sounds or movements, the background plant life, and even the page borders all illustrate a basic pattern for children to discover. Patterns vary in complexity from ABAB to ABCDABCD, and conventional notation is explained in endnotes.

Hoban, Tana. *Cubes, Cones, Cylinders, & Spheres.* New York: Greenwillow Books, 2000. **(X)**

In her characteristically inviting photographs, Tana Hoban explores these four shapes in a variety of contexts. Cones are shown as hats, bushes, and roofs; spheres appear as bubbles, lights, and hot air balloons; cylinders become smokestacks and drums; and cubes are depicted as blocks and dice.

Hoban, Tana. *Look Book.* New York: Greenwillow Books, 1997.

Color photographs of the natural world are seen through a circular hole in the page and then viewed in their entirety on the next page. The author features dandelions, the feathers of a pigeon, the rings of a pretzel, etc. The book is an invitation to look closely at the world.

Hoban, Tana. *So Many Circles, So Many Squares.* New York: Greenwillow Books, 1998.

> The photographs in this collection give a fresh perspective on circular or square objects. Close observation of the pictures can lead to numerous explorations in geometry.

Jenkins, Steve. *Looking Down.* Boston: Houghton Mifflin, 1995.

> In this wordless picture book, a series of illustrations shows the Earth from afar and then progressively zooms closer. The book ends with a view of a ladybug as seen by a kneeling child with a magnifying glass.

Johnson, Stephen T. *City by Numbers.* New York: Viking, 1998. **(X)**

> Stephen T. Johnson inspires readers to observe the urban landscape with fresh eyes through his beautiful, detailed oil paintings. The shapes of numerals are suggested by objects, such as the tops of two garbage receptacles that form an 8. His *Alphabet City* (1995) shows the shape of each letter of the alphabet in the same setting.

Marshall, Janet. *Look Once, Look Twice.* New York: Tichnor & Fields, 1995. **(X)**

> Here is an alphabet puzzle book that features patterns found in the natural world. The author fills each letter with a particular pattern from a fish, flower, fruit, or other object, and readers must combine the pattern and the letter to discover what the pattern comes from.

Paul, Ann Whitford. *The Seasons Sewn: A Year in Patchwork.* Illus. Michael McCurdy. San Diego: Harcourt, 1996. **(X)**

> Twenty-four quilt patterns highlight historic events, daily activities, and other aspects of pioneer life over the course of four seasons. Information about pioneer life and the art of quilting is included.

Pelletier, David. *The Graphic Alphabet.* New York: Orchard Books, 1996.

> The shapes of letters *A* to *Z* are cleverly used to show the meaning of each word on the page. So an *A* crumbles under the weight of an "avalanche," a *G* appears as a cog and a "gear," and an *I* surfaces as an "iceberg."

Rau, Dana Meachen. *A Star in My Orange: Looking for Nature's Shapes.* Brookfield, CT: Millbrook Press, 2002.

In this beginning book for young readers, the author uses color photographs to show different shapes and patterns in nature, such as stars, branches, hexagons, and spirals. It depicts a variety of a particular shape, such as the star in an orange, a starfish, a snowflake, and a daisy.

Ross, Catherine Sheldrick. *Squares: Shapes in Math, Science and Nature.* Illus. Bill Slavin. Toronto: Kids Can Press, 1996. **(X)**

This book highlights a wide range of activities for grades 3–6 students, such as folding paper puzzles, printing with squares, solving tangrams, and building three-dimensional shapes. It also discusses the use of squares in architecture, including city designs, buildings, and houses. Other excellent books in this series include *Triangles* (1994) and *Circles* (1992).

Rotner, Shelley, and Richard Olivo. *Close, Closer, Closest.* New York: Atheneum, 1997. **(X)**

Perspective and scale are introduced to readers through pictures of objects taken from three different distances. The book features a strawberry, feather, butterfly wing, coins, mitten, and other objects. It invites readers to look for patterns using a magnifying glass.

Sandved, Kjell B. *The Butterfly Alphabet.* New York: Scholastic, 1996. **(X)**

For more than twenty-five years, nature photographer Kjell Sandved traveled around the world in order to find 26 species of butterflies, each with a letter shape on its wings. Each double-spread consists of a rhymed couplet, a full picture of the butterfly, and a close-up of the letter shape on one wing.

Steele, Margaret, and Cindy Estes. *The Art of Shapes: For Children and Adults.* Los Angeles: Museum of Contemporary Art, 1997. **(X)**

The authors use contemporary pieces of art (both paintings and sculptures) as examples of basic shapes as well as of stars, hearts, and spirals. Images include oval fruits by Matisse, rectangular suitcases by Jacob Lawrence, and sculptural cones by Claes Oldenburg. The book can be a springboard for looking more closely at pattern and design.

Swinburne, Stephen R. *Guess Whose Shadow?* Honesdale, PA: Boyds Mills Press, 1999. **(X)**

This basic informational text explains how shadows are formed, and the accompanying photographs reveal a variety of interesting patterns of manufactured and natural shapes. The pages that invite children's participation in guessing what object creates a pictured shadow might inspire children to create their own similar books.

Thong, Roseanne. *Round Is a Mooncake: A Book of Shapes.* San Francisco: Chronicle Books, 2000. **(M, X)**

As a little girl discovers round, square, and rectangular shapes in her urban environment, she is reminded of her Asian as well as her American heritage: round rice bowls and round pebbles; square dim sum and square pizza boxes; and rectangular Chinese lace and a rectangular pencil case.

Tompert, Ann. *Grandfather Tang's Story.* Illus. Robert Andrew Parker. New York: Crown, 1990. **(M)**

Using seven tangram pieces to create the animals for his story, Grandfather Tang narrates the tale of two fox fairies who always try to outdo each other. The fairies chase each other by transforming themselves into birds, squirrels, crocodiles, etc. Readers are encouraged to predict what new animal will appear before turning each page.

Walter, Marion. *The Mirror Puzzle Book.* Norfolk, England: Tarquin, 1985.

In order to solve each of these twelve advanced puzzles, readers must study a boxed-off figure and then place a mirror (provided) on the lines of symmetry of twelve other figures to match the target shape. At least one figure in each set, however, has no solution because, as the author explains, knowing why something doesn't work is just as important as understanding why something does work.

Williams, Rozanne Lanczak. *Mr. Noisy's Book of Patterns.* Illus. Kathleen Dunne. Cypress, CA: Creative Teaching Press, 1995.

Everything that Mr. Noisy does—sing, dance, talk, drive—makes patterned sounds. Emergent readers will want to join in reading the text and echoing the sound effects.

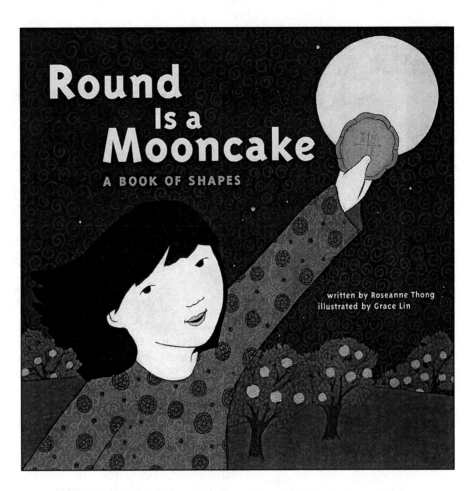

Classification

Baer, Edith. *This Is the Way We Go to School: A Book about Children around the World.* Illus. Steve Björkman. New York: Scholastic, 1990.

Children around the world go to school in different ways: by bus, car, ferry, roller skates, cable cars, horse and buggy, skis, trains, and more. Locations of these places listed at the end of the book invite further research.

Giganti, Paul Jr. *How Many Snails? A Counting Book.* Illus. Donald Crews. New York: Greenwillow Books, 1988.

A series of questions invites readers to classify and count the objects pictured in Donald Crews's bold, bright illustrations. The word *and* is used mathematically to specify attributes of a given set. Children can use a similar questioning pattern to create their own books.

Grejniec, Michael. *What Do You Like?* New York: North-South Books, 1992.

> In a simple text with warm and imaginative illustrations, a brother and a sister tell to each other their favorite cat, fruit, music, and more. This is a book that invites the graphing of children's favorite foods, games, pets, and so on.

Jenkins, Emily. *Five Creatures.* Illus. Tomek Bogacki. New York: Frances Foster Books, 2001.

> A young girl describes the three humans and two cats that live in her house by classifying them according to a variety of attributes. In many cases, humans and animals share a characteristic, such as the love of climbing trees (the two cats and the girl), thus demonstrating the flexible use of classification schemes.

Jocelyn, Marthe. *Hannah's Collections.* New York: Dutton, 2000.

> Hannah describes her many collections, from Popsicle sticks to barrettes and feathers, as she ponders which to bring to school for a special project. The brightly colored mixed-media collages of Hannah's interesting arrangements will encourage readers to sort and display their own collections.

Nozaki, Akihiro. *Anno's Hat Tricks.* Illus. Mitsumasa Anno. New York: Philomel, 1985.

> Classification necessitates logical thinking, so we have included this book here. In a series of increasingly difficult puzzles, Tom, Hannah, and "Shadowchild" (represented only by its shadow) use clues given by the narrator to identify the color of their hats as red or white. Readers must use clues and deductive reasoning to determine the color of each character's hat.

Reid, Margarette. *A String of Beads.* Illus. Ashley Wolff. New York: Dutton, 1997. **(M, X)**

> A young girl and her grandmother sort beads in a variety of ways and make necklace patterns. Endnotes provide information on how different cultures used beads for decorative and religious purposes.

Appendix A

Additional Experiences with One-Half and Other Fractions

1. How many different ways can you cut a square in half? Try a rectangle. How many different ways can you cut other regular polygons in half (equilateral triangles, pentagons, hexagons, octagons)?

2. Fold a square into two rectangles. Can you fold it again so that the rectangles become squares? Continue to fold it and record what you see.

3. In what different ways can we cut food in half? Does it matter how we cut certain foods in half? With which foods does it matter and with which does it not matter? What does the inside of certain fruits look like when we cut them in half in different ways?

4. In what different ways could the piece of cheese in *Two Greedy Bears* be broken into two unequal pieces (e.g., 1/4, 3/4; 1/3, 2/3)? Draw and illustrate as many different ways as you can. What do you notice about your answers?

5. What if the pieces of cheese were *almost* half but not quite? How many ways can you show two fractions that are almost half? Look at all your fraction pairs and decide which pair is closest to being halves. How can you tell?

6. How could the two bears divide equally two unequal parts? For instance, what if they first broke the cheese into 1/4 and 3/4? How could they then divide those pieces so that each bear would have the same amount? What if they first broke the cheese into 1/3 and 2/3? How could they divide those pieces into two equal shares?

7. How many different ways could the cheese be broken in half (e.g., 1/2 + 1/2; 3/6 + 3/6; 4/8 + 4/8)? What if the cheese were broken into thirds or fifths? How could the pieces be shared? How would you describe the pieces that each bear would get?

8. What if the cheese were broken into two unequal pieces (such as the answers in item 4) and each bear decided to divide each of those pieces in half? Then each bear would have half of the small piece and half of the larger piece. Would they have the same amount? How would you describe the pieces that each bear has? Try this out for several of the answers you obtained in item 4. What do you notice?

9. What if the fox dropped the cheese and it broke into the 7 tans known as "tangrams"? How many different ways could you show two halves with these 7 pieces? (See Figure A.1.)

Figure A.1
Tangram Puzzle Pieces

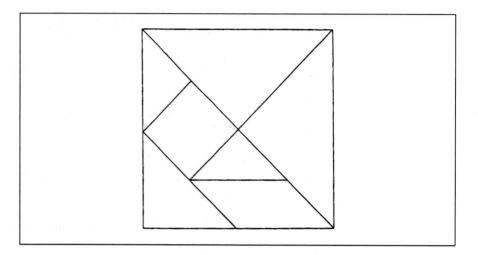

10. Make a square. Fold the square horizontally and vertically. Connect the midpoints of each side. What shape did you create in the middle? How does its area compare to the area of the entire square? How can you prove this? What will you find if you try other squares? Will this work with rectangles? Parallelograms? Equilateral triangles?

11. Use one-inch cubes to make different rectangular blocks of cheese. How many different ways can you divide this block in half? Do the halves have the same dimensions? Do they have the same surface area? Try different rectangular blocks and see what you find.

12. The largest pizza ever baked was 100 feet and 1 inch in diameter and was cut into 94,248 slices. How would the bears have divided that pizza pie in half?

13. Following are some statistics involving one-half and doubling. Use these statistics to do some of your own calculations.

   - A person's height at two years of age is about half his or her adult height.

   - About one-half of a person's weight is water.

   - Less than half of the average person's body weight is muscle.

   - The average newborn baby usually doubles its weight in six months.

   - If bacteria are given food and a warm, wet place in which to grow, they can double their number in about one hour.

14. What if the bears found $1.00 in coins? How many different ways could the bears divide the coins so that each bear received one-half (e.g., 5 dimes for one and 2 quarters for the other; 40 pennies and 2 nickels for one bear and 1 quarter, 15 pennies, and 1 dime for the other, etc.)?

Appendix B

Transforming Rectangles into Parallelograms

1. Use the geoboard and rubber bands to make a rectangle (Figure B.1).

2. If the small square on the geoboard represents 1 square unit, how many square units are in this rectangle? (Answer: We can say it has an area of 2 square units.)

3. Now stretch this rectangle into a parallelogram by moving the top bands to the right by 1 nail (Figure B.2).

4. What is the area of this parallelogram? (Answer: 2 square units)

5. Stretch this parallelogram into one that appears to be slimmer by moving the top bands to the right once more (Figure B.3).

6. What is the area of this second parallelogram? (Answer: 2 square units, using the sides as diagonals of rectangles)

7. Try stretching rectangles of different sizes into parallelograms and see what you notice. Why do the areas remain the same?

Notes

When rectangles are stretched (mathematicians call this stretching "shearing") into parallelograms, the areas remain constant. This surprising result (children often predict that the slimmer parallelograms will have less area) is because the base and the height of the parallelogram remain the same as in the beginning rectangle. In this case, the height is 1 unit and the base is 2 units. After testing out this shearing on other rectangles (including squares), children can deduce that the formula for the area of a rectangle ($b \times h$) can also be applied to parallelograms. They can reason that any parallelogram can be transformed into a corresponding rectangle with the same base and height.

Figure B.1
Figure B.2
Figure B.3

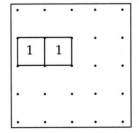
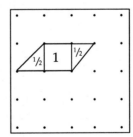
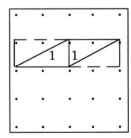

Appendix C

Exploring Pentominoes and Building Cubes

1. Take 5 one-inch squares and see how many different shapes you can make by arranging them with their sides joining. Two ways are considered different if one cannot be made to fit on top of the other. If two shapes can be made to fit on top of each other, they are congruent, and the shape can only be counted once.

So this:

is not different from this.

And remember, sides must be touching completely. These are not permitted:

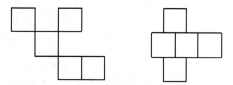

2. Record the different arrangements on inch-square graph paper.

3. How many different arrangements did you find? There are 12 possible solutions, called "pentominoes." They are listed below:

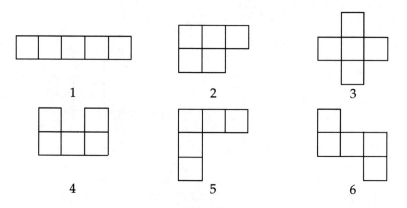

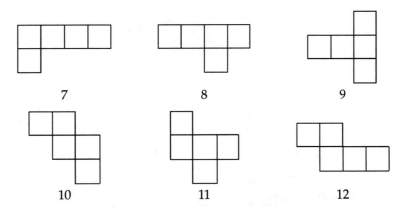

4. Now imagine a box, all of whose sides are square. Take the top off this box. How many sides does your box have now? Each of your pentominoes has 5 sides too. Which of your pentominoes do you think could be folded to make a box without a lid? Make a prediction list of which ones will be box-makers and which ones will not be box-makers. Now find out by folding them. (Answer: Only 1, 2, 4, and 5 are *not* possible.)

Notes   This activity is an introduction to the process of making three-dimensional shapes from two-dimensional patterns, or nets. It emphasizes that the faces of solids are plane figures. One way to extend the activity is to challenge children to find all possible arrangements using 6 tiles, known as hexominoes. There are 35 solutions. Students can then predict which of these arrangements can be folded into boxes *with* a lid.

Appendix D

Discovering Lines of Symmetry in Regular Polygons

1. Cut out a circle. How can you find its center without measuring? (Answer: Fold it in half twice.) How many ways can you fold a circle in half? (Answer: Infinite folds)

2. Now try to fold an equilateral triangle in half. How many ways can you do this? (Answer: 3 folds) What about a square? (Answer: 4 folds) (See Figure D.1.)

3. What do you predict for a regular pentagon, a regular hexagon, and a regular octagon? ("Regular" refers to polygons that have equal sides and equal angles.) Test out these other shapes. What do you notice? (Answer: The number of lines of symmetry are equivalent to the number of sides of the given polygon.) Folding these shapes to make two congruent halves helps mark the center as well as highlight lines of symmetry.

Figure D.1
Lines of Symmetry in Regular Polygons

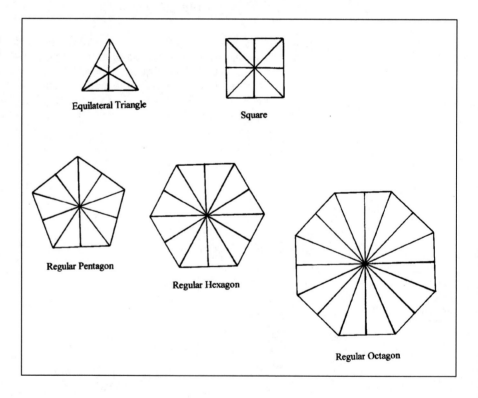

Equilateral Triangle

Square

Regular Pentagon

Regular Hexagon

Regular Octagon

Appendix E

Investigating the Rotational Symmetry of Regular Polygons

1. Have children trace and cut out (on cardstock) the following regular polygons: equilateral triangle, square, pentagon, hexagon, octagon.

2. Be sure that they mark each angle of each shape as well as its corresponding window:

Window of cutout
equilateral triangle

Actual cutout of
equilateral triangle

3. Have students place the shape inside its window and then lift it up and rotate it so it fits back in the window.

4. How many times can they rotate an equilateral triangle until they return it to its original position? (Answer: 3) What about a square? (Answer: 4) Now try a regular pentagon (Answer: 5), a regular hexagon (Answer: 6), and so on. ("Regular" refers to polygons that have equal sides and equal angles.) Thus, a square needs 4 rotations to make a complete revolution. Discuss with the children the fact that every angle of the square (and of the other regular shapes) fits into every angle of the window. This exact fit underscores the equivalence of these angles. If there are 360 degrees in a complete rotation, then how many degrees are there in one rotation of a square? (Answer: 90) What about a regular pentagon? (Answer: 360/5 = 72) A regular hexagon? (Answer: 360/6 = 60) Such an investigation helps students determine the number of degrees in the interior angles of these regular polygons.

Appendix F

Comparing the Areas of Circles and Squares

1. Make four different-sized squares on centimeter paper.
2. Inscribe a circle inside each of these squares.
3. Find the area of each square and record it on a chart.
4. Find the area of each circle. Invent a way to count partial squares as well. You want to try to be as accurate as you can.
5. How much of the area of each circle is inside the area of each square? How can you find out? (Answer: Divide the area of the circle by the area of the square.) (See Figure F.1.)
6. Find the percentage for each square/circle example.
7. Find the average of these four percentages.
8. What did you find? We see that the area of a circle is about 79 percent of the area of the square circumscribed around it.
9. So another way to determine the area of a circle is to use the following formula: A is approximately $d \times d \times .79$ (d representing the length of the diameter of the circle). Squaring the diameter is a way to find the area of the circumscribed square. Then finding 79 percent of that square yields the area of the inside circle.

Figure F.1
The Area of the Circle Is Approximately 0.79 of the Area of the Circumscribed Square

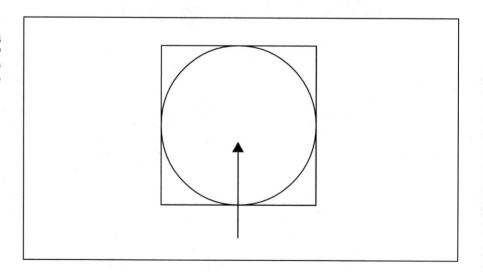

Authors

David J. and Phyllis Whitin are both faculty members at Wayne State University in Detroit, Michigan. David teaches mathematics education and general curriculum courses. A former elementary school teacher and principal, he has always had a love for both language and mathematics. His previous work in the area of mathematics and literature includes *Read Any Good Math Lately?* (1992); *It's the Story That Counts* (1995), coauthored with Sandra Wilde; and *The Magic of a Million* (1998), coauthored with David M. Schwartz. Phyllis teaches courses in children's literature and language arts, drawing on her wealth of experience teaching preschool through middle school. As a fourth-grade teacher, she was invited to teach a demonstration lesson for the PBS Elementary Mathline Project. Her interest in literature response and visual representation is reflected in her book *Sketching Stories, Stretching Minds* (1996).

The Whitins have conducted collaborative research in elementary classrooms for many years. They are both interested in inquiry-based instruction and integrated curricula. They have coauthored articles for both mathematics and language journals, as well as two books: *Inquiry at the Window* (1997) describes the integration of science, mathematics, and language; *Math Is Language Too* (2000), which focuses on the role of reading and writing in mathematics classrooms, was the first copublication by NCTE and NCTM.

This book was typeset in Avant Garde and Palatino by Electronic Imaging.
Typefaces used on the cover were Berkeley, Bodega Serif, Eidetic Neo, Myriad Condensed, and Zapf Dingbats.
The book was printed on 50-lb. Accent Opaque paper by Victor Graphics, Inc.